WON

WITH

PURPOSE

WON

WITH

PURPOSE

POSITIVELY IMPACTING LIVES
ON AND OFF THE FIELD

ANDREW LIMOURIS

Published by Advantage, Charleston, South Carolina.
Member of Advantage Media Group.

ADVANTAGE is a registered trademark, and the Advantage colophon is a trademark of Advantage Media Group, Inc.

Printed in the United States of America.

ISBN: 978-1-59932-693-1
LCCN: 2017931851

Cover design by Katie Biondo.

This publication is designed to provide accurate and authoritative information in regard to the subject matter covered. It is sold with the understanding that the publisher is not engaged in rendering legal, accounting, or other professional services. If legal advice or other expert assistance is required, the services of a competent professional person should be sought.

Advantage Media Group is proud to be a part of the Tree Neutral® program. Tree Neutral offsets the number of trees consumed in the production and printing of this book by taking proactive steps such as planting trees in direct proportion to the number of trees used to print books. To learn more about Tree Neutral, please visit **www.treeneutral.com.**

Advantage Media Group is a publisher of business, self-improvement, and professional development books. We help entrepreneurs, business leaders, and professionals share their Stories, Passion, and Knowledge to help others Learn & Grow. Do you have a manuscript or book idea that you would like us to consider for publishing? Please visit **advantagefamily.com** or call **1.866.775.1696.**

To my family, both at home and at Medix, and all of the coaches, teachers, and mentors who have helped me on my journey to finding purpose.

TABLE OF CONTENTS

FOREWORD

I've been spoiled working with Andrew Limouris and the Medix team.

As a business coach, I'm a really big believer in purpose-led cultures and thought I had been part of creating truly purpose-led companies…until I met Andrew.

He is someone who *lives* purpose deeply and intensely, and through the pages of this book, you are about to catch a glimpse of the impact he has experienced every day in his company, in his community, and as a coach.

This is purpose on a wholly different level.

When people first meet Andrew, they're not quite sure about him because he's a giant ball of energy, and it can be hard for a lot of people to get their head around—until you realize he is the real deal: a heart-driven, purpose-led leader.

Everyone talks about purpose, how it's important, how they lead a purpose-led life and business. But the reality is that most just don't measure up to what I've experienced with Andrew and his organization. He's like an elephant compared to an ant, energetically and intentionally charging in to have a positive impact on people's lives, every single day.

When he got the news that the father of a kid on an opposing football team had died in an accident, he immediately left our planning session to collaborate with the other coaches to find some way to honor him.

He helped build a monument near a sports field to honor a little girl who had passed away after a battle with cancer.

During retreats, instead of going out to dinner or to play golf, his executives will go to a nursing home to read mail to residents and listen to their stories.

He invited the maid who cleaned our villa at the Mexican resort where we were on a company retreat to join our trip to an orphanage, and he didn't think it was a big deal. We took books and toys and he asked what else we could do. That led to new bedding, soap, two dentists to care for everyone's teeth, and carnival games for fun.

There are too many stories to tell.

But the depth of his purpose really hit home for me one night at the home of a wounded army veteran in Scottsdale, Arizona. Andrew and his company had not only helped raise the money for a house for the veteran and his wife (through Jared Allen's Homes for Wounded Warriors) but members of his team had even showed up to roll up their sleeves, put on some work gloves, and put the finishing touches on the landscaping. And the executive team returned one year later when invited to a backyard BBQ. I watched Andrew as we listened to stories of what the veteran had been through and witnessed Andrew's deep and sincere interest in the life of this veteran and his family that went beyond what he and his company had already done. The veteran was so moved by Andrew that he gave him one of his treasured military coins.

After that, I was well past a theoretical understanding of what living a purpose-led life means. I was in the middle of it, and it changed me. Andrew brings that engagement, that passion to his life and his business.

When you scratch beneath the surface of most people's accounts of passion, there's nothing but a good story. When you scratch beneath the surface of Medix and Andrew, there's more—so much more that it scares people. He's a machine in the way he wants to makes a difference in people's lives and has built an organization to have a positive impact on others, not to win, to look good, or for a marketing slogan or a PR campaign.

His story is about responsibility, an unstoppable force to help others that comes from a deep appreciation of all the people who showed up for him. Without them, he says, he wouldn't be where he is today. And so he pays it forward.

This book is for anyone exploring purpose—deep, meaningful purpose. If you are a leader in your community, in business, or elsewhere, and you really feel a desire to make a difference in your part of the world, this book is for you.

—Kevin Lawrence, strategic advisor and coach to Medix and other CEOs and business leaders across North America and internationally www.coachkevin.com

ACKNOWLEDGMENTS

In writing this book, there were many people who played a key role in the conception and evolution to whom I would like to express my gratitude.

First, I would like to thank Jordan McGuire. Jordan was definitely my rock during this book-writing adventure. This book would not have come to fruition without her guidance, organization, and true wisdom around the details. Jordan is a true example of someone that leads with purpose in business and also in her personal life.

I would also like to thank the mentors outside of the organization, such as our executive coach Kevin Lawrence and the members of our Medix Advisory board, who have worked with us and have not only helped shape who we are as a company but provided guidance throughout the book-writing process to ensure the purpose of the book itself rang true with Medix.

I would have no story to write if it wasn't for the exceptional personal mentors mentioned in this book who have shaped who I am as a coach, professional, and person, such as Coach Engen, Jody Roy, Bob Gibson, and the numerous others that are the true foundation of this book.

Of course, I owe infinite gratitude to my wife, Maria, for her continued focus on the conscious impact of the book as well as those involved. Just like our relationship, she helped me throughout the book process to keep me grounded and real.

I can't thank Lynn Allaway enough for her creative genius and exceptional writing skills throughout the book-editing process, as well as anyone else on the Medix team, in the community, and beyond who I tapped on the shoulder to read the book and provide me candid feedback and advice. A very special thank you goes out to the Gadomski family for not only their willingness to impact the book with advice and counsel but for allowing me to share the story of Caitrin and the everlasting impact she will have on me and countless others.

I also wanted to recognize the entire Medix team. Not only did many of them provide stories that are included right in the book, they are the lifeblood of the organization, and without the wonderful people who make up the unique culture that is Medix, there would be no book.

In the same vein, I also wanted to thank all of the coaches with the Golden Eagles program and the rest of the league living the same purpose and values, the players, and their families, both for providing stories for the book but also for teaching me so many lessons in life and leadership for me to share throughout this book.

THE PROFOUND POWER OF PURPOSE

If I told you that I jump out of bed every morning, anxious to start searching for ways to positively impact people's lives, you might think I'm exaggerating. Okay, the idea of leaping out of bed *every* day might be a little overstated, but I am someone who truly values the opportunities that I have to do good in the world. And those opportunities are plentiful because, you see, in addition to being the CEO of a successful company with locations in multiple cities, I am also a husband and father, a son and brother, an in-law and a friend, a youth coach and a mentor. In short, I'm someone who believes strongly in being present in life, of being more than just a member of a community. I want to have purpose in everything I do, and that purpose is to positively impact the lives of the people around me.

Thankfully, my professional path has put me in a position where the ability and opportunity to drive true impact is literally around every corner. Medix is an international staffing organization specializing in recruiting and placing talent in the healthcare, scientific, and information technology industries. We excelled from the infant stages of our business and fared well even against the headwinds of the

1

2008 economic downturn. I'm not saying we didn't have a few tough times along the way, but we've managed to grow revenues to over $170 million without any debt or private equity investors. Today, we're an organization doing business in more than forty states and Canada and employing more than 350 internal teammates. In 2015, after more than a decade in business, we hit a milestone that only a small number of companies (about 0.5 percent) ever reach: $100 million in annual revenue. According to Staffing Industry Analysts (SIA), an even smaller number of staffing companies (about 0.008 percent) ever reach that goal. To say we are an anomaly is quite an understatement.

So how did we achieve this? Admittedly, during its early years, Medix was about winning and achieving traditional metrics of financial success. We felt we had a culture of cohesiveness and compassion, but we experienced high turnover and, as with many businesses, our steady growth came with its share of challenges and missteps. But even back then we were tinkering with the idea of "our purpose": what were we truly trying to accomplish on the human scale? Beyond dollars and cents for the company's bottom line, what was in it for the people we employed, the people we served, the people whose lives we affected every day? We always knew we wanted to do something to help others, but in 2012, we finally formalized our mission—our purpose—to have a positive impact on other people's lives.

Since we've begun articulating and engraining our core purpose, we've seen dramatically positive effects on turnover, productivity, and teammate engagement. We've transformed the company in ways we never anticipated, and it has been a source of motivation for our teammates, our talent, our clients, and our communities.

For me, discovering Medix's purpose has also profoundly affected my personal life. I now approach partnering, parenting, coaching youth sports, and every human interaction from a completely different place.

I wanted to share this journey because I strongly believe that discovering Medix's purpose wasn't isolated to just the company. Discovering purpose resonates on a deeper level, deeper than dollars and cents and revenue, deeper than winning sports games. I believe that when you operate your business, forge your relationships, run your teams, and live your life truly with a core purpose in mind, you will reach true personal contentment and professional success. Whether you win a championship, hit a revenue or margin milestone, unite a team, or build a company, when you follow your purpose, you will win.

CHAPTER 1

IT'S ALL GREEK TO ME

I grew up in a tight-knit, blue-collar, Greek immigrant family. My parents were born on the island of Zakynthos and immigrated to America in 1970 before my brother and sister and I were born. None of my family spoke any English. When my parents moved to the states, Dad started working at a small, retail wholesale baking company. Our house was a white 1,200-square-foot Cape Cod "castle" in Appleton, Wisconsin. It was humble, but it was home.

Our family, transplanted straight from the Greek islands to the middle of America's farmland, stuck out like a sore thumb. At a barbecue, when all the other parents would bring burgers and potato salad to pass around, my mom's Greek goulash got a couple of side glances. My parents' thick accents prompted my friends to sometimes even prank-call my house just to hear my mom talk. It wasn't as if people threw rocks at our windows or anything; I just always felt different. I would never pick a different place to have grown up. My family made many genuine friends in the community, and they really embraced and appreciated our American citizenship, proudly flying the flag outside our home. The experience of being from an immigrant family gave me a different perspective on life that I carry with me to this day.

When I was in grade school, my mom had a janitorial job at an insurance agency, the Aid Association for Lutherans. Her shift ended around 9:15 p.m., and my dad and I would sit in our family Pontiac to pick her up, patiently (or impatiently) waiting for her to finish while listening to "Top 9 at 9." I loved to see how her sorority of coworkers exited the building together and bid each other goodnight with big hugs. My mom was the only immigrant in the bunch. She cleaned bathrooms and offices for a living, but it was a job that gave her a sense of self-worth; she was helping to support her family. If you were to judge from the smile on her face at the end of her shift, you would have thought she had just finished changing the world, not scrubbing toilets. That's the sense of purpose she had in her career and life. At the same time, she cherished the camaraderie of American workmates who understood each other so well. They were all close friends, and they couldn't wait to see each other at work each day.

My dad, on the other hand, didn't have that shared sense of camaraderie at work. He managed a bakery and, as the boss, he certainly cared about the people who worked for him. He also cared about the quality of the products and the reputation of the company. He put in grueling eleven-hour to twelve-hour days in front of a hot oven. But at the end of the day, the business was more of a means of making an income to support his family, the people he was happy to come home to. Even back then, I knew that work required dedication like my father's, but I also wanted a fulfilling career that let me experience the sense of camaraderie and purpose I saw in my mother's career.

I remember my first bout at kindergarten (yes, I said my *first* bout). I wasn't at school very long before they pulled me out. I just wasn't ready; because English wasn't spoken at home, I wasn't where the other kids were academically. I needed to go to prekindergarten to help me get up to speed, but I never truly felt I had caught up. All through grade school, I noticed I learned differently from everyone else. Things didn't click as easily for me, and I had trouble reading. By third grade, my frustration was mounting. I noticed I was a year older than all of my friends in the same grade, and I would get pulled out with four to five other students for special classes. When I didn't understand things, I would grow embarrassed and upset. I remember saying, "This sucks," out of frustration with an exercise I didn't understand in fourth grade and getting suspended for it. I needed an outlet outside the classroom where I could experience success.

To me, sports are the ultimate equalizer. They meant I had something I could actually excel at. In the classroom, I was picked last and put in a separate room; on the football field, I was picked first. People looked at me differently. I began to truly crave team sports for how they made me feel. What I didn't expect was the profound impact it would have on who I would become.

When it comes to teamwork, winning, and purpose, I credit my early experiences in football for shaping the man I am today. As a youthful observer and wannabe, then a player in high school and college, and finally a youth sports coach, I learned so much from this game.

The first lessons I learned about "purpose" came at a very early age. Before I was ten years old, I hung around the high school football field, watching my big brother, Nick, play. Paul Engen was the head football coach at Appleton West High School at that time. From my vantage point on the sidelines, I thought he was the best high school football coach in the nation.

I was in awe of Coach Engen, his assistants, and the team, and I wanted more than anything else in the world to someday wear that blue and orange jersey and play football for the Appleton West Terrors. In retrospect, I would come to understand why Coach Engen's style resonated with me so much, but at that youthful age, all I knew was that I wanted to be part of what was happening right in front of me on the field.

Sometimes, during games, I got to be a ball boy, but most of the time during practices my enthusiasm just equated to pestering, and when I got underfoot too much, I'd get an earful. Still, Coach Engen and his staff got to know me pretty well before I was old enough to play on the field.

My antics continued into high school when it was finally my turn to play on the team. Within the coaching circle of Coach Engen and his assistant coaches—Gruber, Sukow, Smrecek, and Weinberg—I earned the nickname Wingnut since I was always going a mile a minute. Thank God that nickname did not spread outside of the coaching staff to my teammates. I went out of my way to act the clown, and my mouth was always running, often making me the center of attention. Looking back, I think I was overcompensating for my lack of self-confidence. Even though I was verbose (extremely, as the adults would have told you), I continued to struggle through my studies. And as a lot of kids were, I was undisciplined.

But that all began to change under Coach Engen's guidance. As a member of the team, I learned focus and discipline and the value of teamwork. But they were painful lessons in those early days. Coach Engen insisted on a commitment to excellence with the focus always on the team, never on individuals. I didn't truly get the meaning of what he was teaching, however, until my junior year when he benched me for half a game.

That week, during practice, he pulled me aside and told me I would not be playing the first half of the game on Friday. Away from the team, but with the other coaches in attendance, Coach Engen told me in no uncertain terms that I was a screw-off, essentially letting me know that I wasn't adding value to the team with my behavior. Why? Because I didn't respect myself, he told me. "And until you do, no one else will respect you either," he said.

His words stung. I sat in that little office, angry, confused, and slightly embarrassed. Under the Friday night lights, Coach Engen had me follow him up and down the field with my helmet buckled through the entire first half. Mortified and antsy to return to the field, I walked the sidelines instead, watching as my teammates competed out on the field without me. The game ticked by, each minute growing heavier as I filled up with anticipation to get out there and make my contribution to the team and do what I loved. After the first half, Coach Engen looked me dead in the eyes and said, "Are you ready to play?" As I ran onto the field that night in the second half, my eyes were brimming with tears. During that second half, I played my heart out. I left all my energy on the field, but the lessons I took with me from that night stay with me to this day.

Suffice it to say, even with Coach Engen's words ringing in my ears, it still took some time to get the goofball in me under control. As a teenager, I wasn't conscious of my purpose, place, and impact. That is not something that happens overnight. I still have a fair amount of goofball moments, but I'm okay with that. People don't seem to change; they just learn to become the best versions of themselves. Thanks to Coach Engen's tough love, I learned to preserve the things that made me unique but to calibrate the goofball side of me a bit;

when you're more balanced, you can resonate with people better and drive more impact.

With high school graduation looming, I pegged myself as going to a community college. And then I met Coach Bob Nielson, the head coach at Ripon (currently the head coach at the University of South Dakota). Coach Nielson did an incredible job of recruiting players from my high school team. He recruited four players for the team's upcoming season, including me. Until then, I had never been formally recruited. I had never met with a collegiate coach. Coach Nielson took a lot of time during the recruitment process to not only get to know me but also my family. Once I had heard Coach Nielson's magnetic presentation, I knew I wanted to play for him. And he wanted *me* to play for *him*. First, however, I had to get reference letters, write an essay, and get accepted to the school. I asked Coach Engen to write one of my reference letters because he could speak of things I was good at and my work ethic. I believe that my acceptance to college was due to Coach Engen and the others who advocated on my behalf because, with my ACT scores and GPA, there was no reason I should have gotten in. But there it was, one day in the mail: my acceptance letter to Ripon College.

I wish I could tell you that I never took this opportunity for granted and devoted myself to being a model student and earning that acceptance from day one; however, I did not. I made a lot of wrong decisions during my first couple of years at school. On my breaks from college, I would go back to Appleton to work my summer job and join Coach Engen and his staff as a volunteer coach, and the exposure to this environment still had a positive impact on me. But back on campus, embarrassingly, I was more invested in my social life than in education. I got a 1.67 GPA in my freshman year.

Instead of earning the acceptance letter I felt I had not deserved in the first place, I earned myself a spot on academic probation.

I decided to stack my academic chips in the speech communication department, thinking that it was going to be a blow-off major. I still had not found my confidence and didn't trust that I could handle rigorous academic courses. I was wrong about it being a blow-off major, but thank goodness I made that decision. I would end up meeting another key mentor who would shape not only my path to graduate college but how I would go about living my life, even to this day.

Under the guidance of Professor Jody Dalton (now Professor Jody Roy), majoring in speech communication was anything but a "blow-off." She took no excuses and always demanded the best out of her students. The coursework was rigorous and demanding for everyone, not just me. Right from the start, Jody had this manner that let her students know she *cared*. She *believed* in them. Her curriculum was tough, but her teaching and coaching style made her students feel welcome and inspired them to lean into the challenge.

This didn't mean I wasn't still struggling. When my actual academic skills fell, my lack of confidence dragged me down even further. For one of Jody's exams, I earnestly studied very hard. I knew the material, yet I still didn't trust myself to be able to pull it out of my brain on test day. My brilliant plan was to write words in the bill of my hat that would trigger me to remember the concepts. They weren't the actual answers—this was an essay test—but rather key words. It was enough to catch the eye of Jody, and she grabbed me on my way out of the classroom.

"What was that?" she asked. "I don't get you. You know this material. You do not need to cheat." She ended up giving me the same exam orally, and I nailed it. I had just been too intimidated to articulate my answers on paper. I radiated confidence on the football field, but my lack of confidence in the classroom only amplified my weaknesses. Jody still gave me the F grade I deserved that day, but by demonstrating to me that I actually knew the answers, she gave me a tough lesson in believing in yourself. It also helped me begin to confront my struggles head-on and discover what the true roots were. The "difficulty reading" I had experienced in elementary school was officially diagnosed as dyslexia in college. By facing and diagnosing my challenges, I was better equipped to overcome them myself.

Most people recall important developmental milestones throughout their youth into early adulthood. I can say with complete certainty that the lessons I learned through football, school, and the angels in disguise whom I met along the way are what truly set the course for my future and my endless pursuit of meaning and purpose.

CHAPTER 2

FINDING MY PURPOSE

After college, I made the decision to head back to Greece. As many immigrant families have, when we were kids, we had the opportunity to visit my parents' hometown, the island of Zakynthos, in the summer. The lush green of the island was reminiscent of the spring of the Midwest, and the smell of the sea and the boats floating in and out of the harbor mesmerized me, a child used to the farmland of rural Wisconsin. At night, the island came alive with dinners, laughter, and the enchanting lights of the town illuminating the hills. I was so taken by the culture and landscape of Greece I decided that, as soon as I graduated college, I would head there to find a job, convinced that was where I would stay.

I landed a sales job with a distributorship that sold paper products, hand creams, and suntan lotion throughout Zakynthos. Turned out I had a knack for sales: I truly wanted to do what was right for my clients, and I loved building relationships with them and gaining their trust.

But after about six months, I came to realize that I was actually working in an old-world, Southern European environment. Greece, at the time, had a pretty solid business climate, but backroom deals happened daily. My values were completely misaligned with the business climate and those of the company I worked for. There was a lot of infighting among the family owners of the business, and it seemed that everything benefited the company and family first. Sure, I was young, but even then I felt that teammates are members of the company's team, and there really was little, if any, regard for teammates' welfare in that organization. I just knew there had to be a better way to run a business and to treat the people who contribute to the bottom line.

In the fall of 1995, I returned to the United States and joined a staffing company where my brother, Nick, worked. He convinced me by saying, "Andrew, you are the only guy I've ever known who can talk three or four hours on the phone and love it." (Yes, when I was a kid, my parents constantly had to peel me off the phone.) My brother pointed out that, as a recruiter for a staffing agency, I'd be spending a lot of time on the phone, getting to know prospective candidates. So I interviewed and was hired to help recruit technical personnel and to work in the customer service and administration departments.

I was part of a team of coworkers—all in their early twenties—who had a contagious work ethic. We came early, stayed late, and worked together as a cohesive team. It was almost cult-like. We'd all be in at 7:00 a.m., refilling our coffee cups time and again (even though we didn't *truly* like coffee), in part to mimic the leaders in the organization and also out of necessity just to make it to the end of the day, when we would all loosen our neckties and head out for happy hour or a group dinner. Then we would sleep, wake up, and do it all over again. It was perfect for someone like me, someone who found the greatest motivation in being part of a group working toward a common goal.

During these early staffing days, I met my incredible wife, Maria, when I was out with some friends. We happened upon a Greek restaurant when a group of young women walked in for a birthday party. I was immediately drawn to Maria. She was beautiful, for sure, but her smile was completely infectious. We didn't exchange numbers that night, and I thought I'd never see her again. Two weeks later, she walked back into the same restaurant and passed her pager number along to the waiter for me (yes, her pager number). And the rest, as they say, is history. Ever since, she stood by my side, challenged me to be my best, and supported my career. I remember Maria showing up at my promotion party after I had earned a position in sales. She brought a cigar and a cigar cutter for me to celebrate with the team. She always believed in me and my dreams, right from the start, no matter where the twists and turns would take us.

Over the next few years, I had three jobs in HR departments at technology companies. During my time at the second company, I was in an executive meeting providing an HR update, and the president was expressing pain around having too much overhead in the HR department. I brought up a business idea I had, which was to create a revenue-generating HR department. We were receiving three times more resumes than we needed. We could place those applicants elsewhere and generate a profit. The president was excited by the prospect of this idea and encouraged me to start drafting up a business plan with the CFO and the executive director of HR. I spent the next six months drafting this plan, but by the time it was finished, the company was preparing to be sold. I was left with a business plan and nothing to do with it. I moved on to my role at the third company with the plan still in my back pocket, but then

9/11 hit. Due to the economic downturn that followed, I ended up losing my job.

It was officially time to firm up that business plan and put it into motion. It was going to take all hands on deck. Because of the financial uncertainty we were experiencing during this time, Maria and I moved into my father-in-law's home; my sister-in-law and her family also moved in three months later. Talk about a full house! I remember the whole family sitting at the kitchen table, one night, talking about the business plan and kicking around company names. It was actually Maria who came up with the name Medix. I decided to pull the trigger, and Medix was incorporated on January 24th, 2001.

With a name, an investment from my father-in-law, and a tiny executive office space, Medix was officially born. The support from my family during this time was invaluable in getting the company launched. Having my father-in-law Louis's backing not only afforded us the investment we needed to start the company, but his support throughout our early years of business allowed us to run really fast, hire great people, and grow. We could be more aggressive, which was important to our ability to scale early in Medix's history.

I couldn't have asked for more supportive parents. I remember picking my mom and dad up from a little condo they were renting at the time. We filled up my vehicle with office supplies, cleaning supplies, and an insanely large Gateway computer that took up my whole desk. Our first office wasn't the classiest of executive office spaces, and it was a bit grungy and dirty. Given my mom's profession, she took great pride in her ability to clean just about anything, and she made that space look as nice as possible. My dad and I kept going back and forth from the office to the car, unloading supplies. By the time we had emptied the car and walked back inside, my mom had already found a perfect place for everything. She made me look like as much of an executive as I could.

After putting on the final touches, we turned to walk out of the office. My mom stopped, looked at me, grabbed my face, and said, "You have my blessing. Work hard and everything is going to go well." The look in her eye was almost like she knew something—like she could see the potential and the vision and knew how it would all end up. This affirmation meant the world to me.

The environment of a brand-new company is electric—and terrifying. There was really no downtime. Workdays would start at 7 a.m. and finish at 9 p.m. We were literally running around all of Chicago, trying to build a company. My wife was just a saint during this time. Not only did my work take me away from my family but we were living under my father-in-law's roof, and my wife was pregnant with our firstborn, Denin. Talk about patience.

When Denin was born, the company was in full development mode. As if being a brand-new father and a brand-new CEO simultaneously was not trying enough, things were about to get even tougher. My parents had moved back to Greece by this point. I had received word that my mom, who had been suffering from pancreatic cancer, had taken a turn for the worse. I packed up and left my newborn and my wife at home to head to Greece to see my mom. The doctors told us that at this point, there was nothing left that they could do to reverse her condition but that my mom wasn't in a state where they felt she could handle that candid of a conversation. I remember getting her out of the hospital and wondering to myself how much she truly understood what was going on. At her home, I showed her pictures of her new grandson. "You need to go get back to your wife and baby," she had said. I remember as we pulled away from the house on that trip to head home, I pressed my face up against the car window and peered back at the house, wondering if that was the last time I would ever see my mother.

After returning from Greece, life back home was chaotic, to say the least; I have no idea what I would have done without my amazing support system. In addition to trying to deal with the stress of a growing company, my days were also filled with anxious calls with my father to see how things were going with my mom back in Greece, and my nights were filled with the cries of our newborn baby. The weight of trying to be the best husband, new dad, and CEO I could be while simultaneously trying to cope with my mom's condition was getting the best of me. I remember being in a meeting with a client once and spontaneously bursting into tears halfway through, excusing myself from the room. I was a wreck.

Then, one day, I received that dreaded call from my father; we needed to get back to Greece immediately if we wanted to say good-bye to my mom. My brother and I hopped on the first plane we could to head to Europe. We did everything we could to get to the port in time to make the last ferry to the island that night, and we *just* missed it. The next ferry was at 6 a.m. I didn't sleep at all that night. We found a tiny inn to stay in, and I remember clutching a little journal I had with pictures of the baby in it and little notes jotted down of things I wanted to make sure I said to my mom before she passed. I knew in that moment my brain would be jumbled. I didn't want anything to be missed.

At 6 a.m., we got on the first ferry out. I hopped into my uncle's car and begged him to hurry up. I noticed he was driving the opposite direction of the hospital. When I asked him what he was doing, he burst into tears; I immediately knew my mom was already gone.

The time that transpired after that was a complete blur. I remember wondering how on earth we were going to go about planning a funeral after this; my company was in its infancy stages, I had spent most of my money on my new house and had no cash, and emotionally, I didn't know up from down. My father-in-law Louis then did something I will never be able to repay him for. He gave me $5,000 and said, "Go ahead and give your mom the funeral she deserves." It made it so I didn't have to cut any corners. He showed up for me when I needed it most.

Returning to America and to work, after dealing with the funeral arrangements, I felt like a shell of a person. I was not emotionally prepared and for months could barely function. When I walked into the office, disheveled, with a full beard, and still in complete shock and bewilderment, my team stepped in. They told me not to worry about it. They would handle the business. "Don't worry. We've got your back," they told me. "Take as much time as you need." They had my back and helped me get on my feet during one of the most trying and chaotic periods of my life. When it comes to coworkers, you spend countless hours of your life with these people. During this time, I learned what it truly meant to have a family both at home and in the office. I don't know how I would've gotten by without *both* of these safety nets catching me at one of my lowest points.

OUR UNIVERSE EXPANDS!

I was fortunate enough to have a team that not only helped us merely survive during those trying times but persevere and grow. As the company progressed, an opportunity for expansion presented itself leading up to 2004, when we landed a substantial client. We discovered an internal champion at this account, someone who has always believed in Medix, our business model, and our work ethic. She has continuously given us opportunities to earn more business and expand into new markets.

One of those opportunities was in Scottsdale, Arizona, where we had just a handful of mini contracts. By early 2005 I felt I needed to be in Scottsdale on a daily basis to set this office up for success and lay down the framework for Medix to continue creating opportunity on a national scale. This would mean moving my whole family from the Chicago area to Scottsdale.

These plans were complicated by the fact that Maria and I were about to have our second child. We decided to hold off leaving Chicagoland until the baby had been born because the due date was so close and all of Maria's doctors were in that area.

On April 11, 2005, our son Eli was born, giving our first son, Denin, a sibling, and making Maria and me very happy parents for a second time. After three days in the hospital, we returned to my father-in-law's house to settle in with our newborn. As everyone was calling to check on Eli and offer us their good wishes, Maria's motherly intuition kicked in: she noticed he looked as yellow as the color of my book.

We took Eli to the pediatrician, Dr. C (who happened to be our client as well), who sent us down to the lab to have blood work done. We were sitting and waiting for the results when Dr. C called my cell phone and asked, "Where are you right now?" I told him we were in the lab waiting room. "Do you know where the pediatric intensive care unit is?" she asked. "I'll meet you there. Go right now," she ordered. Filled with anxiety and questions, Maria and I immediately stood up and headed to the PICU. We turned the corner, and two nurses were waiting to take Eli. As young parents, one of the most frightening things is to have your newborn suddenly whisked away, leaving you with empty arms and a lot of questions and waiting on pins and needles for the results. It took two nurses to hold Eli down for the testing (that's when we knew he was going to be a fighter).

A hematologist came out to deliver us the results. Eli had G6PD a red blood cell deficiency and was going to need to be in isolation in the PICU for treatment. The doctor went through the risks. "AIDS through blood transfusion, mental retardation, mortality . . ." I felt numb just thinking about it.

What amazed me was the overwhelming support from the Medix team during this time. It was unbelievable how many people stopped by the hospital or called to check on Eli's well-being. They really had my back during that trying time, the same way they had a few years earlier when my mom had passed away. This really taught me the true meaning of having someone's back and "showing up," in good times and in bad. My team will never know how much their support—in big actions and small—impacted me during these times.

Eli recovered a couple of weeks later, and Maria and I packed up our boys and our belongings and headed to Scottsdale. We moved our family into a house that hadn't been lived in for about a year and was overridden with scorpions. It was quite the transition, but we were able to make it due to the team of stellar leaders and all-around fantastic people that made up that Arizona team.

Things changed after Scottsdale. An unintended consequence of moving to a city like Scottsdale is that everyone we hired was from somewhere else. And as a result, we became a family. You know how, on some forms, you have to fill in the name of your emergency contact? Well, we became each other's emergency contacts. In Scottsdale we became more like peers. We all worked together. We came early, stayed late, and went to events together outside office hours. We had barbecues and celebrated birthdays and anniversaries. We even celebrated the special days of our extended family members. It became a much more collaborative environment and reminded me of an infinity symbol, in which everything just continually flows and loops back again; family flows to work, work becomes family, in a continuous loop.

It would be many years until I could put a name to this sense of family beyond blood, to this commitment to having one another's back. It is this sense of family, this hunger for pursuing unified goals and truly trusting the brother or sister next to you that is the core ingredient for every Medix office we have opened ever since. It is this that has afforded us the opportunity to open Medix offices coast to coast, increasing our national and international footprint and impact while retaining the unique qualities that allow us to grow as individuals, as a company, and as a family.

CHAPTER 3

EVEN COACHES NEED COACHING SOMETIMES

Throughout our various stages of growth at Medix, it was clear to me that the organization was still in major development mode and we needed to scale. While we maintained steady growth, I still felt as if my hair were on fire. I had an overwhelming sense of what Jim Collins calls "productive paranoia." I was fixated on the idea that we could not let up and that we could always improve. Just as in football, if we were winning by a landslide at halftime, we would go into the locker room as if the score were 0-0. I don't think I'll ever be completely satisfied knowing there is always something more we can do. To achieve continued success, you have to be relentless.

If we wanted to continue down a path of growth and success, I knew we would need a true coaching methodology around accountability and business development. Now, as someone so involved in sports, I knew the importance of coaching to a playbook. If you're going to run a three-four defense, a four-three defense, or a five-three defense, there's a playbook so the players know what to do. If you're going to run a jet offense, a double-wing offense, or a spread offense, there's a playbook. You have methodologies and priorities when you manage a team. But we didn't have them at Medix. We would embark on this or that tactic or plan willy-nilly; there was no true playbook. We tried some new tactics at our offices in Scottsdale, Arizona and Lombard, Illinois, but those ideas could not really gain traction without a defined play. Over time, we as a company discovered the importance of playbooks to outline our processes and strategies for success, the notion of truly defining what your objective is and laying out the steps to get there. But even with defined plays, you need someone to hold you accountable to them.

Finally, it dawned on me, after my experience of both being coached and coaching on the football field, that in order to alleviate our lack of disciplined systems and processes, we might be able to benefit tremendously from having an executive coach to help us navigate.

Since we had originally built the company by recruiting people we knew, some of the key people on our executive team were people I started my career with. One was a referral from a friend's younger brother from way back in elementary school, and another was a friend from high school. I thought there would be great value in having a confidential and supportive partner who would be honest about our strengths and challenges. I knew that an experienced, professional executive coach would bring objectivity to the table and prevent too much group thinking. We needed someone who could help facilitate the transformation I sensed we needed to scale and move forward, someone to bring us perspective, provide structure, and impose accountability.

My first inclination was to call Kevin Sheridan from my college fraternity, who was running a human resources solutions practice. He was a Harvard grad and had written a couple of books—a very sharp guy. We spoke about engagement, and I invited him to give our leadership team a presentation on it. Later, we tried one engagement tactic he suggested: stop—start—continue. We'd ask teammates what we should stop doing, what we should start doing, and what we should continue doing. We got a couple of nuggets from that but nothing substantial. We rarely closed the loop by getting back to people about their recommendations, and when we did, the feedback was vanilla at best. Kevin's suggestions were spot on; we just needed to find a more effective way to execute.

In truth, at that time, our executive team was not ready to get serious about engagement; we were still more interested in growing revenue. We did not understand the concept that "revenue is vanity; profits are sanity," meaning that the money you bring in can be a shiny number to throw around but is not what you actually net, your true value. We were hell-bent on continuing to grow. All that mattered was the impact on the bottom line. We didn't always understand the full impact on people.

Then I went to a staffing industry conference where Verne Harnish, author of the popular "Growth Guy" economic strategy column, was speaking. At first, I thought he was going to be just another ho-hum speaker. Sometimes it's hard to know how applicable and effective the message will be at these events. But he started talking about the key to growth, the importance of a one-page plan, and the methodology to organize a fast-growing company through rhythm and accountability. He was talking about having a playbook and the importance of a coach to guide you through those plays. He was speaking my language.

Because of the way he spoke, I felt I was the only person in the room. As I sat there, listening to him, I thought about how we were operating. Our meetings didn't always go smoothly. There was no methodology to scale the business or to prioritize our to-do list.

I was so inspired by his speech that, after it, while the rest of the audience was applauding him, I made a beeline for the stage to be the first in line to talk to him. I asked him to recommend an executive coach who could work with my Medix team.

Soon after that, he contacted me and introduced me to his team, and we eventually began to interview coaches.

We engaged our first outside coach in late 2008. He began to work quarterly with our executive team and was a perfect executive coach. Coach Les was disciplined and calm, and he brought a sense of order and focus to our team. He created a vulnerable and open environment, which allowed us to set the table and dive into the challenges we were facing and start down the path to scale our business. He gave us a much-needed, fresh perspective. For the first time, at our executive meetings, we had a moderator who guided a structured agenda and who held us accountable for quarterly tasks and results. He introduced formats and methods we had not used before. We put together quarterly one-page plans and financials for review at each quarterly meeting. We set goals that quantitatively defined what success would look like to us. Getting organized and imposing accountability at Medix in this way was a first for us and it felt right.

After a couple of years, Coach Les, who had been commuting to and from Toronto, decided he needed to confine his client base to Canada. We felt sufficiently versed in the new process to proceed on our own.

"In between Les and Kevin, we went through a coachless phase. We were young and thought we'd learned the ropes and could do the coaching ourselves. We named a moderator and made that person accountable for making sure we stayed on task, challenged each other, and had, overall, productive meetings. We quickly learned that this wasn't something we could do ourselves. Having an outside perspective to keep us focused on the big picture was a necessity."

—Mike, Director of People and Performance, Medix

It actually worked for about eighteen months, but over time, it became clear that, naturally and unintentionally, individuals came to these meetings with their own agendas. In an environment like that, it can be easy for conversations to be biased and circular. That year reminded me of a football team trying to win a game without disciplined coaches to implement strategies and tactics. It was much easier to end up with honest outcomes that were best for the company when we had a facilitator helping us all speak the same language. We decided it was time to call in another executive coach to help us strategize, plan, and implement more effectively.

That's when Coach Kevin Lawrence came to us, and he has been with us ever since. Coach Kevin is more than a facilitator; he feels like a member of our executive team and Medix family. He is detailed and disciplined. He challenges us and makes us question our motives, and yet he is as vulnerable with us as we are with him.

He openly shares personal and professional challenges and triumphs. He takes the time to get to know the very core of Medix. We really get the sense that he has our back. Coach Kevin is truly part of the Medix team, from going with our executive team to an orphanage in Mexico, to enjoying a cookout with us at a wounded veteran's home that we helped build. He is in complete alignment with our mission.

"Prior to having an executive coach, we had a vision of where we wanted to go but lacked the road map to get there. Coach Kevin, along with the Gazelles methodology, has provided us the tools to effectively run our business and identify what we should be focused on in the short term (ninety days), mid term (one to five years), and long term (the big hairy audacious goal—BHAG). There is an increased level of discipline and accountability that starts at the executive level and cascades through all levels of the organization. I am confident that our will-ingness to listen to a coach and stay consistent with this methodology will provide the framework to hit our goal of having an impact on twenty thousand lives and more."

—Jared, VP of Sales, Medix

I cannot overstate how much of a difference, more than anything, having an executive coach has made to Medix. I would highly recommend one for every business organization. Coach Kevin has especially shown us the importance of having a tight cultural fit within the executive team, with teammates, and throughout the organization as a whole. The difference between our executive meetings before and after bringing in a coach has been astounding. Our coaches have brought a formal agenda to the efforts of our team. Having an executive coach for your business is like having an offensive coordinator walking you through every conversation, keeping you on track and organized, all while cheering and encouraging innovation within the specific skill sets that exist in your company.

Our executive coaches have ingrained a culture of accountability that is necessary to meet our goals for scaling the business. Our executive team has adopted the Gazelles method, which involves meeting to review quarterly goals and our annual one-page plan to ensure it remains in alignment with the needs of our fast-paced business. In addition, our executive team members check in with each other three times a week for fifteen minutes to flag any issues that need addressing. All of our salespeople, professional recruiters, and leaders gather annually for a company kickoff meeting. And our office leaders meet quarterly to agree on messages to communicate to teammates in their respective offices across the country.

We also have a rigorous touch-point system to promote our accountability agenda. Entire office teams gather for ten-minute meetings (which Medix calls FasTrak meetings) three times a day to confirm the day's priorities and reprioritize if necessary. FasTraks are also an opportunity for team members to reach out to other teammates if they need assistance with a task.

When you are selecting an executive coach or consultant, it's important to find someone who really understands your culture and helps you find a methodology of accountability that works for you. Find somebody who will challenge the status quo, who's not afraid to tell you how things are done elsewhere.

Coach Kevin, for instance, brings that outside view, but he doesn't push too far because he "gets" us. Take our philanthropy, for instance. We place a huge emphasis on philanthropy, which some might see as distracting from the business. But Coach Kevin knows this is something we're not budging on. It's our core purpose, and it's what we're going to do. So he works it into our plans while helping us to keep it in check.

In my experience, investing time and energy in finding the right coach for your team can be critical to your success. Find someone who not only understands your culture but also your quirks and your goals, both in the office and in your communities. Find someone who is comfortable enough with the team and your processes to hold you accountable to them. You'll be able to run faster and keep your eye on the ball as a true high-performing team.

BACK TO THE FIELD

The rapid expansion of a company affords many opportunities to refine coaching skills, but I yearned to get back into coaching in my personal life as well. In 2009, I decided to try my hand at helping coach my son's second-grade flag football team. I learned that everyone has a passion, whether it's participating in team sports or playing in a band or acting on a stage. But for you to be even better at your passion, whatever that is, you need the care and compassion of mentors, people who want to see you succeed in your goals. In my case, those people were Coach Engen and Jody, and I made it my goal to be that person for someone else. Good mentorship is something to pass on. When you have the ability to lead, you really must use that ability to give back to others. At the time, I was one of the few coaches who had actually played the game at the college level on a competitive, organized team.

When I first took the field as a coach, my experiences as a competitive player were the ones I carried with me. So naturally, since I was approaching it backward, I thought the goal was to win. These were seven- to nine-year-old kids, and here I was trying to get them to understand how to outsmart the other team's players! I didn't realize that the goal was to parent them as much, if not more, than coach them. My role was to be supportive, not push winning, and reinforce good team behavior and collaboration, but it took me a while to figure that out.

Instead, there I was, in the last game of that season, driving the kids as hard as I had throughout the whole season. I was acting as if that last game were a championship game. I was yelling out instructions and being overly aggressive and competitive as I tried to get the kids to run plays and to run here and there. I made it about me, not them.

After the game, the grandfather of one of the players came over and let me have it. I was walking to my car with my family when he walked right up to me.

"Did you ever play this game?" he asked me, pointedly. I let him know I had played in both high school and college. "Are you trying to overcome your own failures on the field through these kids or what?" he asked. "I played football myself, and let me tell you, I will never let my grandson play for you again. This isn't how you treat kids. You have a chance to impact them, and this is the wrong way to do it."

For a minute there, I felt I was back in the locker room with Coach Engen and all the other coaches when he read me the riot act in my junior year. The grandfather chewed me out in front of my wife, kids, and all the other parents. I can still hear the man's booming voice.

Walking with my wife to our car, I kept shaking my head and saying, "I can't believe that grandfather acted like that. Here I am, a volunteer coach. I'm not getting paid for this. I'm trying to help these kids. I can't believe this. I just can't believe it."

I easily could have disregarded his words and kept my ego intact. Yet, for the next few months, his words haunted me. I played them over and over in my head until, one day, I finally grasped what he had said to me. He was right: my job was to know my audience. If I had, I would have realized that my role was to make sure they had fun. These weren't high school kids competing for the state championship. They were little kids. Their only desire was to have fun playing football. To them, that was winning.

I am so grateful that grandfather had the courage to confront me and hold that mirror up to me on the football field. He could have simply gossiped or complained to his family about the "awful football coach," but he confronted me when he knew something wasn't right. For that, I am truly thankful. Transparency and honest feedback can be difficult to give—and even more difficult to receive—but they are imperative to personal growth.

I learned many more valuable lessons in coaching during my time as an assistant coach to Bob Gibson. Coach Gibson was a veteran coach with the organization but new to this particular team. During the first week of working as the defensive coach with Coach

Gibson, I discovered that somewhere along the way, I had fallen back into that mode of wanting the game to be about winning. It's not that I hadn't learned my lesson from the last time I had coached kids, but this time around, the kids were playing tackle football, and they were a little bit older—ages nine to ten. Plus, I was pumped because it was my son's first time playing tackle football, so I wanted to teach the kids about proper tackling, various plays, playing safely, and all of the fundamentals of the game. And I was psyched to put together a good game plan, good defense, and good offense.

Coach Gibson, meanwhile, put together five plays and a basic defense. He wanted the kids to write a one-page paper about why Troy Brown of the New England Patriots was a good teammate, which they had to read aloud to the team. What? First of all, I was a Green Bay Packers fan (obviously, Bob was all about the New England Patriots), but a paper? Really? When it came time to present the papers, Bob got all these ten-year-old kids on their feet and shouted out, "Stand up. Suck in your stomach. Stick out your chest. Don't mumble. You have to be loud. You're not eight or nine years old anymore. You're ten-year-old young men." One by one, the boys would come up to present—to present their papers, to present their thoughts, and to present themselves.

What Coach Gibson was teaching was discipline. Not only did they write papers during the year—no double spacing to lengthen a too-short essay, by the way— but they learned

a few dozen plays, which was more than I would have ever expected! And they were a good team, maybe average by comparison but with vastly improved performance because they had learned discipline.

Besides writing papers, Coach Gibson taught discipline through other tactics. At practice, when the kids were going to get a drink, he'd say, "Pots off, gentlemen. Get a drink." None of the players ever sat on his helmet or tossed it. They would line up their helmets in single file while Coach checked them. If they were not in single file, the players would have to run across the field and do push-ups. It was all about discipline, even in the little things. And when he said, "Pots on," the kids had five seconds to put their helmets on or they'd have to do push-ups. I do the same with my football team to this day, "Five, four, three, two, one…on your bellies!"

Practice was as much about learning how to be accountable for yourself as it was about football. Coach Gibson used to tell kids in the eighty-three-pound league (players weighing a maximum of eighty-three pounds): "If you're sick, you still need to show up at practice before you go home and look me in the eye and tell me, 'Coach, I'm sorry. I'm sick. I'm checking in, but I need to go home.'" If the kid had something contagious, he was allowed to call in, but the player had to make the call himself.

It was truly amazing to watch those young boys turn into responsible young men right before my eyes. At first, the kids were a little bit uncomfortable with this new coaching style. Over time, you could see them take ownership of themselves and their actions. That motivated them, and I saw in them a growing sense of pride in being responsible for themselves. The best indicator of the difference in the kids was how they showed up and presented themselves, their ability to initiate and maintain eye contact, and their increased confidence. At the beginning of the season, you saw kids looking down and speaking softly. By the end of the season, they looked you directly in the eye, and you could see their confidence and ownership of themselves as individuals, which was a truly magnificent thing.

The discipline was off the charts. I'd never before seen a coach doing this stuff. But you have to know your audience. This was youth sports. What were we trying to do? We were trying to develop awareness in these young kids that we hoped would carry with them into adulthood.

"With the leadership of the coaches, the kids learned the value of teamwork. If one player made a mistake on a drill during practice, the entire team would repeat the drill. Steven made every practice, every game, and tried his hardest to remember every homework assignment. It was important to my son because he never wanted to let his 'brothers' down. We smile knowing that as our son grows older, eventually applies to college, gets his first job, and starts his own family someday, he will have a strong work ethic, understand the importance of teamwork, and know that, to achieve a goal, he must work hard to make it happen."

—youth football parents Scott and Colletta

Coach Gibson also liked to say things such as, "If you do the little things right, big things will come." My own youth coach, Coach Engen, had similar sayings, including "If you're disciplined, great things will happen." The lessons they were instilling were more than dealing with the here and now; they were instilling values in young people that would be useful to them down the road. It can be difficult for anyone, especially children and even young professionals, to overcome the desire for immediate gratification or return on effort. Kids don't always understand the process of investing energy that won't be returned to you until the future. "If I worked really hard in practice yesterday, how come I didn't make that catch?" It is a tough lesson to engrain.

Coach Gibson and Coach Engen delivered the same message to youth football players that I hear from business consultants all the time: take care of the details and big things will happen. I take the same approach with new teammates at Medix. They are encouraged to take on challenges, and they are supported by their mentors. If you coach people to reach for goals, whether they are kids or adults, it's amazing what they can accomplish. In the right environment, you can scale fast.

The lessons I took from these experiences corrected my approach to coaching and mentoring and eventually shaped the way I and the entire coaching staff approached the season when we ended up winning the league championship, which they call the Super Bowl. Whether it was transferring these lessons to later football seasons or back to the boardroom in my role as CEO, even when you are a coach yourself, there is still so much to learn from the individuals you encounter throughout your life.

"At the end of the day, I look for three characteristics in any youth sports season. Did the boys have fun? Did they learn the proper way to play the game? Did they improve as the year went on, individually and as a team? The last part is not measured in wins and losses, but did the kids play hard and competitively? This season, all of those things were achieved and exceeded expectations."

—youth football parent Nick

CHAPTER 4

BUILDING YOUR COACHING TREE

As the company progressed during its early years, it became apparent that in order for us to continue to grow, it was not enough that I direct the team; we needed to create other coaches and leaders across the organization as well. They say to hire people who are as good or better than you. I had met Eric seven years prior and had worked with him at a previous company. I knew his work ethic and what he stood for. When I was looking to multiply my own team and had discovered that Eric was open to making a career change, I couldn't pick up the phone fast enough. I knew Eric was better than I was, a real A-player, when I brought him on to lead our Chicago office. Before Eric, everything went through me. Looking back, I realize I was pretty overbearing with the Medix staff. My heart was in the right place: I was focused on serving our clients, on seeing they always got incredible service, and I wanted to make sure the talent we placed was always treated with amazing respect. This meant I was pretty hard on internal staff. I expected people to come in early and stay late. I was hard charging. Some of that hard charging was a feeling in the pit of my stomach from my mom's passing. After she had passed away, I became bound and determined to not let her down. I had to make Medix work.

I had an epiphany on how to make it work at a healthcare staffing conference where they talked about the importance of building the right team and having the right people in the right seats. I started to chart out what this winning team would look like and saw it would take a lot more than just me. It would take a true team of many leaders, and I needed to have a strict focus on coaching them.

Because Eric was such a stellar leader, I was able to move to Arizona during those early growth stages to focus on building this coaching tree, knowing Chicago was in excellent hands. During these crucial moments for the company, a number of key people joined Medix and enabled me to begin to step back and really start trusting others. During that first period in Arizona, Jared was one of those people; he had industry experience, and once he was onboard, I was able to step back and begin to coach, to get down on one knee with people and begin to build more than just a boss/employer relationship. During the company's infancy, I had been on the field playing alongside the rest of my team—I was selling and recruiting every day, including on weekends. We were building a sense of trust—a sense that there were others on the team who had your back. For instance, if my son had an activity on a Saturday morning when we had a project going on at work, others on the team who maybe didn't have children would encourage me to go to the event and they'd keep an eye on the business.

Comfortable with the direction of the team in Arizona under Jared, my family made the decision to head back to Chicago. Back in the Midwest, it was time for another milestone. After two boys, Maria and I were about to have a little girl, our daughter Lidia. Everyone was so excited for us to have a daughter; Medix teammates sent gifts like pink Packers gear, and our largest client at the time even came to our house to meet Lidia after she was born (which is a testament to what an amazing partnership we have). Lidia really grew up surrounded by Medix. She had birthday parties with our Medix family, and Medix was like a "second home." When the family would visit the office, she would climb on our teammates' laps to color and "work" with them. When I would be in the office working on a weekend, she would sometimes tag along, writing away on a whiteboard. It means the world to me that my own family considers Medix a "home" and a "family" too.

"What really stuck out to me during my shadow interview at Medix prior to being hired was the fast-paced, dynamic environment fueled by coaching. A talent called in and asked for a certain recruiter, but he was on the other line. The Medix office leader jumped right in and said, 'I'll take it,' and set a great example of how to truly take care of our talent. Also, while I was there, Andrew overheard a conversation a recruiter was having on the phone that wasn't going so well. Afterward, he sat with the recruiter and coached him on the spot to help him handle the situation better next time. Point taken: this is an environment where you will be coached and mentored directly on your own path to leadership."

—Ken, National Director of Care Management at Medix

As we continued to open up offices in other markets across the country, I told myself I eventually needed to get back to Scottsdale.

This was where a huge portion of our business was. I wanted to take control and make sure it was strong. In 2009, the nation faced an economic downturn; with a large amount of business on the West Coast, I was worried I might need Jared to sell again and I might need to assume that leadership role in Scottsdale. We moved back to Scottsdale, Arizona, in December of 2010, right before Christmas. This time, we had to pull the kids out of school in the middle of the year. We had to find all new doctors and everything. But talk about the Medix family—the team surprised us with a Christmas tree waiting in the house! I fully intended to return to the office, roll up my sleeves and get to work. Thankfully, what I experienced back in the office was a team who truly had things under control. The economy started to take a turn for the better, and Jared hired great people to help with the upward climb. Cognizant that I had to let our office leader take the lead, I forced myself to exercise restraint and insert myself only when really necessary.

It turned out to be a fabulous year. We grew by 33 percent, just out of the Great Recession. At a time when most businesses' growth was only creeping back, our Scottsdale office hit it out of the park. I know in my heart this would not have been possible if I alone had been holding the reins. I witnessed our success begin to blossom because we did not have just one coach leading this team; we had several, and they were beginning to multiply.

THE IMPORTANCE OF SELECTING LEADERS

Selecting solid leaders to surround myself with once again translated from Medix back to the football field. After I had spent a couple of years of assistant coaching with Bob Gibson, his work travel schedule forced him to resign from coaching, and he asked me to take the reins for the Golden Eagles.

Fortunately, Bruce Fisher, the offensive coordinator who had worked alongside Bob for many years, said he would continue to work with me even though Bob was leaving. Although he didn't have any children in the program, Bruce coached as a volunteer because he wanted to help develop good citizens and have a positive effect on young people's lives.

Bruce is a lot like Brian, our chief financial officer at Medix. For all intents and purposes, Bruce was our head practice coach. He helped me see my strengths and weaknesses as a coach. Without him, we would not have had the success we did. He was very disciplined and organized. He thought about things no one else did. Brian helps me in similar ways. He keeps an eye on things that I may miss as the CEO. There are countless examples of teammates at Medix who exemplify the importance of surrounding yourself with people who believe in what you are doing but complement your strengths, help you look at things through a different lens, and let you see your blind spots.

When Bob handed the team to me, I realized we needed to add coaching talent. I had previously talked with Pat Donnelley, whose son, Jack, was playing with my son, Eli. Pat had played at the University of Illinois. He was a fun, analytical guy and very smart, very detailed—nothing like me. Pat was also a values-based purpose person. From experience with the games my kids played, his feedback and comments were always meaningful and purposeful. So I asked Pat to coach defense with me. He agreed, and we brought his son to our team. Even though Pat and I were different—he was about the details while I'm more big picture—our strengths complemented each other and we worked well together.

Building a team of coaches on a youth football field was similar to starting Medix and expanding. In each new office, it was important to be sure we had the right leader in place. And that leader needed to be able to build a great team of people who shared the organization's values and purpose. I didn't want clones of myself; I wanted people whose strengths complemented my own.

I always admired the National Football League coaches Bill Walsh and Bill Parcells because they multiplied coaches. They created coaching trees. They made sure their supporting coaches were as good or better than they were so they could scale and grow and give back to the sport. And that's what Bob Gibson did: he grew multiple coaches. This is a key responsibility of leaders at Medix; they are tasked with building coaching trees to develop teams even more talented than themselves.

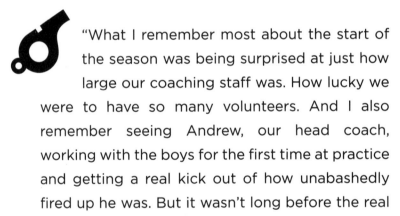

"What I remember most about the start of the season was being surprised at just how large our coaching staff was. How lucky we were to have so many volunteers. And I also remember seeing Andrew, our head coach, working with the boys for the first time at practice and getting a real kick out of how unabashedly fired up he was. But it wasn't long before the real

gift of our team became evident. Win or lose, success or failure, our coaches were positive. Now that might not sound like such a big deal, but if you hang around youth football long enough, you'll witness all kinds of ridiculously bad behavior from coaches. Our boys were being taught how to play in an environment with all the right priorities. It was still football, with all the blood, sweat, and tears, as they say, but for our team there was a higher goal than the win. Yet in the end, we did win. A team that hadn't started the season necessarily looking like a championship team had pulled off an absolutely amazing season."

—youth football parent Kate

FOOTBALL FAMILY MEET MEDIX FAMILY

I've been fortunate to have great coaches over the years. From them I've learned that coaching a team is first and foremost about teaching life lessons. And many of those lessons I've applied at Medix, whether through my own leadership or by introducing the people at Medix to one of my own coaches. I've taken the Medix executive team to meet with Coach Gibson, and I've shared my football team's experiences with them by telling them to see how the ten-year-olds do it because we can learn from them. If that degree of discipline was feasible with kids, there was no excuse for it not to work with a group of seasoned adult executives.

I also had Coach Engen travel with his wife from Appleton to Chicago to speak at our national kickoff meeting in 2008. He talked about what it means to build a team because I wanted our teammates to understand how influential they could be as a coach, a mentor, and a role model in building their own teams. I wanted them to remember that there is no "I" in the word team and to know the value of understanding their role and its contribution to the whole.

I got emotional when I introduced Coach Engen. Here was a man I had admired from the age of six and whom I credit with teaching me very valuable life lessons. Giving him the chance to see how well I'd done was my way of saying thank-you to him for a job very well done. It truly touched my heart to see my football and Medix families merging, to see my teammates being inspired by the same man who had had a profound impact on my personal development. Through the lessons I learned from a championship football coach, I was able to achieve my dream: I too was the coach of a championship team—the business professionals at Medix.

CHAPTER 5

COACHING ACROSS GENERATIONS

"There are lots of stereotypes about millennials: We need instant gratification . . . we feel entitled . . . we need constant feedback every second of every day. Sometimes, we're called the trophy generation because we expect a trophy or gold star for every little thing we do. And some of it is true. We do look at things through another lens. We do seek frequent feedback. What motivates and engages us is not what may have motivated prior generations. But it's not necessarily better or worse; it's just different."

—Jordan, VP of Marketing, Medix

Because of our years of continued and rapid growth, we have always been on a nonstop hiring spree. In our earlier years, we mostly hired people we knew or who were referrals through our various personal networks. We hit a point, however, where I had run out of friends and friends of friends to ask to join the team. (I am only half kidding.) So we turned to college campuses, career fairs, and job boards. Our metrics were the standard ones: build revenue, grow profit, and open new offices. And to do that, we needed to grow our team.

Hiring millennials was an eye-opening experience. One college grad to whom we had extended an offer said, "It sounds great. Would you be willing to have breakfast with me and my dad so he can hear more about the opportunity? Then he can help me make a decision." I found myself sitting at Egg Harbor Café, selling to both the candidate and his dad on the Medix opportunity, discussing benefits and any other concerns or questions they had. In another instance, we had a then twenty-something-year-old call to accept the offer to join our team. I was driving in New Jersey with Jared, director of one of our East Coast offices at the time, and it was pretty late at night. We put the candidate on the speakerphone, and he said, "Andrew, Jared? I just want to give you a heads up that I'm here with my mom and dad and my girlfriend. And I accept the job." We could literally hear him smiling through the phone amid the excited chatter of his family and friends on the other end of the line. Our newest teammate turned his acceptance call into a family party.

I also remember one mother of a teammate we hired in Arizona saying, "You're going to take care of my little boy, right?" It really crystalizes the opportunity and responsibility you have as a coach and leader when you have a mom say something like that to you.

Who knew that some years later, the young man this mom referred to would become one of my closest friends at the company and a senior leader in the organization?

As time progressed, I had more and more experiences with families of these bright, young teammates. I marveled at their competitive, yet oddly collaborative, nature. Work bled into community softball leagues, which bled into happy hours, which bled into charity walks on the weekends. Coworkers bled into friends who bled into a family as vibrant and unique as the individuals who comprised it. It was very clear that these folks were different from me, not better, not worse, just different.

But there is at least one thing that has definitely crossed the generational gap: our Medix millennials work hard. There are a lot of labels out there for millennials, but "lazy" isn't one that can be applied to the millennials in our organization. They're connected by cell phone 24/7, responding to texts at the drop of a hat and connecting with each other—and the world—through the likes of Twitter and Facebook. They appear to be different from other generations, but the truth is they just work and communicate differently at times.

Something else was a real eye-opener for me: the way millennials showed up in force for a cause. I really began to notice this when it came to creating a tribute for a young girl.

Caitrin was a six-year-old girl in our community who was friends with my daughter, Lidia. She was diagnosed with cancer, and despite a fierce fight, she ultimately lost that battle. After seeing photos of Caitrin in the church reception hall following her memorial service and thinking about my own daughter, I was deeply impacted. I was talking with fellow football coaches in the Glen Ellyn program, and an idea sparked. During the service, Caitrin's parents had mentioned how she had loved collecting beautiful rocks. The football coaches and I thought it would be a wonderful thing if our teams dedicated a commemorative rock to her, which we would call Caitrin's Rock. Clemson University has Howard's Rock. Notre Dame has a plaque in the locker room that says "Play Like a Champion Today." Other sports teams had items and symbols that were helpful sources of inspiration and gave teams a reality check on what really matters in life. We thought honoring Caitrin by dedicating a rock in her name could give the youth football team and other area football teams a sense of purpose— much as Medix had—that might help them up their game while keeping perspective. I got behind an effort to lobby the village to approve a site for Caitrin's Rock.

The community of Glen Ellyn held a beautiful ceremony on a Saturday morning in October for a dedication of the rock. To my surprise, nearly two dozen coworkers from Medix, the majority of them millennials, attended the ceremony. These were young people who lived in the city twenty to thirty minutes away and who could easily have been out late the night before or out doing whatever they wanted on their own time on a weekend morning.

They came to the ceremony because they wanted to understand the significance of the rock. At the ceremony, I was asked to get up in front of everyone and talk about what the rock meant. Caitrin was one of my daughter's friends, and across the street from the rock was a park in which Caitrin used to play. The park was basically in her front yard because it was so close to her home. I told everyone that our youth football team had really got behind the idea of the commemorative rock for Caitrin and that, before each game, we honored Caitrin Paige Gadomski's memory and her strength by having every member of the team touch the rock. The intent of touching the rock was to remind everyone how fortunate we were to be able to play a sport and enjoy the gift of life at that moment. And whether we lost a game or won, I witnessed players, coaches, and parents walking past the rock to touch it as a symbol of respect. It wasn't about winning. It was about appreciating the opportunity to even step onto the field.

"Caitrin's story was a significant part of the education our coaches passed on to our boys, and our pregame ritual has inspired this team to fight together in battle and never let each other down. We saw these things physically take shape over the weeks of our season, just as our team and coaching staff were growing together on the field. Early in the season, we saw the orange paint outline the location and eventual home of the rock. Once Caitrin's family selected the rock, we saw the steps taken to place it into the foundation. From there, we came together as a community to unveil the rock in a ceremony. This event allowed Caitrin's family to share their story and teach us the true sentiment behind the battle they faced as a family to fight such a horrendous disease. This inspired the boys to be thankful for the gifts they have and for the time they have together as a team."

—youth football parent Jay

After I spoke at the dedication ceremony, our football team gathered around the rock, and everyone kneeled and placed a hand on it. Our quarterback, probably the most spiritual kid on the team, read the inscription on the rock:

Caitrin's Rock

"Though she be but little, she is fierce."
—William Shakespeare
Live every day with courage and kindness.
Though you may not win all your battles,
give all your effort, and appreciate the
opportunity to compete.

In loving memory of Caitrin Paige Gadomski.

During the ceremony, I saw my Medix family gathered around, releasing balloons and honoring Caitrin with the rest of the community. This began to put things into perspective for me. What had brought them together? *Purpose.* What drove them out that day was their purpose of having a positive impact on lives, giving back to their community, and doing something that made a difference. I was also filled with humility at the realization that they were also out there to support me. The company we had built was one in which all team members supported each other's passions and stepped up to the plate, no matter the situation, no matter the generation.

Another amazing thing happened at the ceremony.

Caitrin had loved rainbows and cardinals and had told her family, "You'll see me when there are rainbows and cardinals." At the conclusion of the ceremony, after her mom, dad, pastor, and others had shared their thoughts—it was a pretty emotional event—we released over a hundred balloons into the air, and as we were leaving the field, someone said, "Hey look!" We all turned around to see a beautiful rainbow painting the sky in the distance.

"The rock quickly became our source of inspiration. Before each of our games, the boys would join hands around the rock and read the quote aloud and realize just how lucky they were to be healthy, to be present, and to be able to compete. It almost seems unreal that, ultimately, our boys went on to have an amazingly triumphant season and win the championship! The combination of everything they learned this season allowed these boys to have a perfect season, a season that they will never ever forget."

—youth football parent and my wife, Maria

PURPOSEFUL POLICIES

The experience of the dedication ceremony for Caitrin's Rock gave me perspective on life, family, sports, and even business. It didn't matter that the teammates standing next to me were from different generations. I knew at that point each one of them was as passionate about purpose and values as I was. And just imagine the impact we could have together.

As we reached the point where the vast majority of Medix's teammates were millennials in their first jobs after college, I began to notice an uptick in differences of opinion. For instance, they wanted to wear casual clothes while I preferred our workforce to dress in business professional attire. They wanted to work remotely, and I wanted everyone on site. They wanted the corporate office to move to vibrant and hip downtown Chicago while I was happy in Lombard, a slower-paced and quiet suburb next to the town I live in with my family.

We decided to implement a weekly, e-mailed, engagement survey program known as TINYpulse. Our HR department releases a one-question, anonymous survey each week. Questions range from the serious, such as "What is one resource that would make your job easier?" to the occasional goofy question, such as "Would you rather have fingers as long as your legs or legs as long as your fingers?" There is also the opportunity to submit a suggestion and a "Cheers for Peers" to recognize your colleagues.

The surveys have been helpful as we work to find a happy medium with the millennials. But while there has been a lot of give and take, there are times when I have to put my foot down. For instance, since 2002, the guys have been asking for permission to grow beards. But we come face-to-face with clients and talent every day, and I want to project a hyper-professional image. I know it sounds harsh, but because Medix has young professionals interviewing and interfacing with seasoned professionals who are sometimes twice their age, we have a professional curve to overcome. I had a hard enough time getting business in my early twenties because youth can be construed as inexperience. I truly feel we have to eliminate any strikes that might be tallied against us. That is simply my belief.

Still, when the requests are purposeful and not just serving a personal whim, then we do our best to accommodate what the millennials on our Medix team want. For example, we compromised on having facial hair by participating in Movember, a men's health awareness campaign. During  November, men across the country grow facial hair in support of men's health and prostate cancer awareness, and we allow our teammates to participate. I get involved myself, growing my best 'stache to support the cause for the month. Teammates across the company have a ton of laughs, poking fun at each other's facial fringe, and many of our teammates, males and females alike, support their teammates' fundraising efforts through donations. The rest of the year, our male teammates need to be clean-shaven.

We have addressed our suit-and-tie dress code in a similar, purposeful way. Medix has been a suit-and-tie environment from the beginning, as that is one of the fundamentals I've felt very strongly about. Why wear a suit and tie every day? Because we're in the business of interviewing people and connecting them to opportunities to impact their lives. We're in the business of sitting in front of supervisors, managers, directors, vice presidents, C-level folks, every day. We're talking to them about their HR solutions, about the talent they need for their organization, and why they're having such a difficult time finding and keeping talent. Whether they're interviewing people to place in an organization, and/or they're meeting with a Fortune 50 company or a small, growing, vibrant start-up that needs folks to build a team, I felt very passionate (and I still feel passionate) that our people should have a suit and tie on. The way we dress is a reflection of how seriously we take our clients and our talent, and it's important we put our best, most polished selves forward.

Then I talked to a leader from another company. He had hired one of our former teammates and knew about our dress code. It was a revelation when he told me, "Andrew, you see the people in our organization dressed up all the time. We're a professional organization. But let's be real. A place that hires millennials can't expect them to come to the office in a suit and tie every day. That just really doesn't work. When young people get out of school, they can't afford five business suits."

That's when I knew it was time to change, and the transformation has been amazing. By altering our dress code a little, we've allowed people to be in an environment where they can dress professionally and still be comfortable, and the result has been happier, more engaged teammates. If they're going to be in front of a client, we still ask them to put on a suit, but there is a bit more autonomy and wiggle room.

In some offices, we've relaxed the dress code to business casual. But there were constant requests to wear jeans on Fridays, so we began accommodating those requests during the month of October with Medix's Think Pink initiative in support of breast cancer awareness. Any teammate who donates to breast cancer during October can wear jeans on Fridays during that month. Our team has taken their engagement with the Pink Fridays well outside the office walls, participating in races and awareness events as a team. Again, we were able to reach a compromise on policies when it was purposeful, to benefit both teammate engagement and our greater communities.

A lot of people think you have to have maximum flexibility on things such as jeans and T-shirts to be able to retain teammates, especially millennials, or that you have to let them skateboard into the office or bring their dogs to work on Fridays. Or you have to be edgy and fun, with beanbags and foosball tables across the office. Maybe those things are deal breakers for some millennials. But in our experience, the reality is that you don't have to do it all. You just need to show good faith by listening to teammates—regardless of their generation—to try to find common ground, to come up with a happy medium. Compromising isn't a millennial thing; it is a generational thing and rather a people thing. Listen to your people. Invest time into understanding their values and aligning your policies with purpose.

CALLING IN THE MILLENNIAL COACH

With millennials, the vast majority of our workforce, I thought we'd come a long way in responding to things they said mattered to them. Through the TINYpulse survey, we allowed for transparency and open communication, relaxed the dress code, allowed telecommuting in a few cases when it made sense, and moved our headquarters to downtown Chicago. But at the end of the day, turnover remained high. Whatever we had done wasn't enough.

The only solution was to fully embrace millennials. They were really at the heart of our drive to succeed, so I made the decision to bring in the "big guns." I wanted everyone in the company to empower each other, regardless of generation, and I became passionate about evolving our culture to one that would satisfy everyone while reducing our turnover.

I turned to Brad Karsh who, with Courtney Templin, had authored the book, *Manager 3.0: A Millennial's Guide to Rewriting the Rules of Management.* After reading this book and seeing the parallels to the dynamics at Medix, I knew I had to reach out to Brad—I mean, he *literally* wrote the book on millennials. I called and told him the situation at Medix, and he asked very detailed questions about the team and discussed his research and his book. His findings fit perfectly into the inflection point where we were at that time. We had millennials. We had millennials managing millennials. His perspective could really help catapult us to tapping into this workforce, if we could just understand millennials better.

I decided to invite him to come and dig in with our executive team. In his first presentation, Brad read an article about a generation of people without identifying the group. The article described the generation as "entitled," "lazy," and "know-it-alls." Then he asked, "Whom do you think I'm talking about?" Everyone said, "Millennials, you totally nailed it." Then he pulled out a *Time* magazine article describing the generation of the people in the room. He showed the year on the magazine: 1996. "No, it's not millennials," he said. "This article was talking about *you*." He explained how this happens to every generation: when people encounter others who work, play, walk, and talk differently, it is natural to get defensive.

Brad proceeded to coach our executive and leadership teams on everything from how to be direct and specific to how to give daily feedback when talking to millennials, as millennials typically thrive on frequent communication. Brad also enlightened us on how much millennials believe in purpose and want their work lives to be associated with something meaningful. Without a sense of purpose, all our concessions would never be enough to get millennials to stay. By championing our purpose, we would finally forge the missing link at Medix; we could really begin to understand millennials, unlock our team's full potential, and continue to grow our company.

With the help of consultants, we also realized that people weren't rallying around our company's goals, in part because those goals had not been articulated. And when it came to those goals, I began to realize that our focus on traditional metrics—the numbers—would only go so far. So I decided that Medix's future success lay in a culture centered on people and relationship excellence. My personal mission became to develop a culture of purpose and human connection at home and at Medix, to figure out why we existed, and to examine our impact on the daily lives of our teammates, talent, and clients.

"Although the boys are a good team, it wasn't their talent that led them to victory; it was their resilience, passion, and heart that, ultimately, led to their success. When playing with heart, the boys were unstoppable. My son's perception on life drastically changed after this football season. As he grows older he may or may not remember his victories and his losses. However, one thing he will never forget is Caitrin's Rock and the lessons he learned from it."

—youth football parent Angelo

CHAPTER 6

DISCOVERING OUR WHY

Instilled with the knowledge that we needed to share our purpose and our goals, our executive team began to explore the concept of discovering our *why*, as formulated by Simon Sinek, author of the book *Start with Why*.

Sinek says there are three organizational tiers: the *who*, the *what*, and the *why*. Most companies put all the focus on the *who* and the *what*. For the longest time, we did too. The *who*: our team, our lifeblood—we said it over and over. The *what*: products, revenue— these are important to us. But there was still something missing. We needed to delve more deeply into the *why*.

So, based on Sinek's model, our executive team went through the exercise of asking why until we couldn't ask it anymore. According to Sinek, you haven't arrived at your purpose if you can still ask why.

Another of my all-time favorite business books is Jim Collins's *Good to Great*. In this book, Collins coined the term *big hairy audacious goal* (BHAG). Our BHAG was always clear: to grow to fifty-four offices and $1 billion in revenue by 2020, but we were less clear on the *why*.

But when we kept asking why, we realized that growing to $1 billion is not a purpose.

So we continued:

- *Why do we want to grow to $1 billion?* To create opportunity.

- *Why do we want to create opportunity?* To see people develop professionally.

- *Why do we want people to develop professionally?* So they can earn money and support themselves and their families.

- *Why do we want them to take care of their families?* Because they spend a lot of time at work. If they spend a lot of time at work—more time than they do at home—we must have an environment that rewards and stimulates them enough to love it.

- *Why do we want to create an environment teammates love?* Because it will motivate them to help talent find opportunities and jobs.

- *Why do we want our teammates to help people find opportunities and jobs?* So we can have a positive impact on more lives.

- *Why do we want to positively affect more lives?*

And that's where we ended. With no more *whys* to answer, we discovered our purpose.

By the way, the efforts worked. By really examining our purpose and our goals and our *why*, we began to understand where we fit in the world, something that related well to millennials and all teammates. And since we have adopted and have begun living our core purpose, we have experienced increased engagement throughout the organization and have had an impact on countless lives. In addition, we have seen numerous tangible improvements in our business in just a few short years since implementing a new purpose.

- Turnover has decreased by over 40 percent.

- Revenue has grown by over 120 percent.

- Net income as a percentage of revenue has doubled.

- EBITDA as a percentage of revenue has doubled.

- Gross margin has improved by almost 10 percent.

"Our purpose to have a positive influence on others' lives has profoundly affected our organization. We broadened our mind-set to focus more on the best interests of talent and clients right alongside the interests of the company and profits. The result of this minor shift in focus has led to increased loyalty from teammates, talent, and clients, increasing revenue and profit and reducing turnover costs. Yes, executing on a purpose to positively affect lives happens to mesh well with who we've always been. Not only has Medix posted consistently strong results during the past few years but many of us have experienced personal growth and reaped other benefits we did not expect."

—Brian, Chief Financial Officer, Medix

It was truly effortless for Medix to toss the obsession with revenue and materialistic metrics and goals to the back burner to focus on our behaviors and who we really sought to be as a company:

- a company giving of resources and time

- a company that would spend Saturdays getting together for a charity 5k

- a company that would get paper cuts wrapping tons of presents for organizations around the holidays

- a company that would take its competitive nature to the food bank, setting competitions for packing canned goods

- a company that would stop a meeting in its tracks to show up, as a team, at the funeral of a family member of one of our teammates

- a company that would laugh, cry, and rejoice over the stories of the impact we were having as a team

As soon as we cleared the path to be who we truly were, the numbers followed.

One of the countless examples that reflect how our purpose exudes from the organization is Amanda's story. Amanda works in our Houston office for our healthcare division. She's been with us for over four years. She and her husband were married only four and a half months when he was diagnosed with a rare form of cancer in his arm. No practitioners in the United States could figure out the best treatment, but it seemed that there was a viable treatment option in Paris, France. As soon as our executive team found out about her situation, we asked what we could do for Amanda. What did she need? We wanted to do our part. In situations like this, it is important for companies to show up for their teammates. We decided to pay for her tickets to France and did not charge her vacation time while she was there taking care of her husband. She gave us updates and we followed up with her husband. The Medix team, both locally and nationally, completely rallied around Amanda and her family. I'd like to think our concern and financial support helped relieve her burden just a little.

"My Medix family has been such a saving grace for us this past year. Without the support from my teammates, we wouldn't have been able to devote our lives to Trent's treatment. The Medix team made sure we knew that whatever happened, they'd be there, and it truly made us feel relieved. Instead of worrying about our work schedules, finances, and so on, we could focus on Trent's treatment. We will never be able to repay Medix for all they've done, but we have promised Andrew that we will pay it forward."

—Amanda, Account Executive, Medix Houston

OUR TRANSFORMATIONAL TOUCHDOWN—ON AND OFF THE FIELD

We had a similar interaction with the power of purpose back on the football field. I coached my son's team from a 4-4 season to a Super Bowl-winning season, not because we were the most talented team in the division but because we found a way to win with our theme of "Together we will." The theme was initiated by Ryan, a high schooler who wasn't able to play on his team that season due to an injury but wanted to stay connected to the sport through volunteer coaching.

He was just a young guy who, no matter if he were playing or not, was drawn back to the field (as was another young guy I once knew).

"The fall 2014 season was my son Denin's fourth consecutive year playing tackle football for the Golden Eagles. Our coaching staff set the tone for the season early: the boys were going to play 'Together we will' football. 'Together we will' football means that the boys play for each other, and they support each other. Not one person is singled out for a mistake and not one person alone makes a team great. The coaches taught the kids how to be passionate, how to be accountable, how to be selfless, and how to be brave. It was really inspiring to see boys as young as eleven and twelve years old learning some pretty amazing tactics that they could not only use on the football field but also in their everyday life."

—youth football parent and my wife, Maria

The team embraced the theme the entire season, each and every practice. The strategy was to get the kids to play for each other, not for themselves. Every single week, we had different activities in which the kids would give speeches about making their "perfect effort" for the player next to them. The whole team knew that to be our best, as a whole, meant locking arms and building each other up. We had a player on our team who was one of the most commanding in stature but who wasn't familiar with a lot of technique. Kids younger than this player helped him run drills to be the best he could be. When we took a knee to huddle, the kids would get so close that they would put their hands on each other's shoulders, almost like a nonverbal "I got your back." The whole unselfish atmosphere made everyone—players, coaches, and fans alike—buy in with full engagement and, essentially, play their best.

As we went into the playoffs, the kids' level of commitment to each other was palpable. Our theme, coupled with the dedication of Caitrin's Rock, produced a profound bond among the team. Sure, the coaches were talking and motivating and doing whatever coaches do, but the kids had bonded together in a way, I would say, was Hoosiers-esque. They started out small and scrappy but bonded and developed, united as a team.

We made it into the playoffs by the skin of our teeth. Our first matchup was against the Bloomingdale Bears, who had already beat us earlier in the season during a hard-fought game on a cold, wet day. The first half of that first game, our kids were getting beat up; Bloomingdale was a more physical team, and they really showed up to play that day. During halftime, I could see our team was deflated. We had some kids hurt and some fighting back tears. Our quarterback had hurt his shoulder during the first half; he took off his pads at halftime and said, "I'm out guys. I'm out for the rest of the game." Morale on the team was completely drained. I took the boys to a pavilion for our huddle to get out of the wind and rain, so we could really level with each other and see if we could get our heads back on straight. Taking the kids up to the pavilion is not a normal thing, but I needed to change the atmosphere. I actually got in trouble after the fact for bringing them there. Our offensive coordinator gave an intense motivational speech, and you could see our team start to get a little more life in them. Our quarterback had even decided to put his pads back on and grind out the second half, reenergized and wanting to get back in there and fight for his team. The team remembered Caitrin's Rock and used that to fuel them, leaning on that message. Even though it was wet, even though it was cold, and even though they were feeling beat up, they were motivated by the fact that they were fortunate enough to even have the opportunity to compete. We ended up losing that game, but we dominated the second half. The kids knew that if we had to face that team again, the game would be ours.

We had that opportunity the first game of the playoffs. Our kids were mentally preparing all week during practice. It was like a scene out of a movie. During water breaks, they'd encourage each other and walk away high-fiving and slapping each other on the shoulders. They were the tightest group of kids I had ever been around. They went into the Bloomingdale game, and from the minute our team touched the field, the kids dominated in every aspect of the game. Our opponents were so surprised when we won that when I came back a couple hours later after the game was done, the opposing coaches were still there discussing what went wrong during the game. They had been completely dumbfounded by the team that showed up to play that day, but I wasn't as surprised; I knew the mental shift that had occurred in them and was sure that when they hit the field that day, it was going to be something special.

The team headed on to the next round of playoffs, where we would go on to play the Tigers, a team that had gone undefeated for two years. We had played them very tough earlier in the year and lost to them as well. The reality was they had some kids that were just plain more athletic than us; we would need to play a perfect game to beat them. And a perfect game we did play (or as close as you can get to it). We controlled the ball the whole time, and every kid played at such a high level. The entire team played with their entire heart that game, not just one or two star players. Again after the game, we knelt by the rock. It had become such an inspiration to them, and it is amazing how at such a young age, they truly embraced it and everything it represented.

By beating the Tigers, the Golden Eagles had earned their ticket to the Super Bowl, where we would face Bartlett, yet another team who had beaten us earlier in the season. They had hit us harder. They had run faster. They really came after us. Every team we faced in the playoffs had beat us earlier in the season, which could be demoralizing for some. But at this point, the team was playing beyond their abilities. They were playing for something more than themselves. Preparing for the Super Bowl that week, I was in awe of the intensity and discipline the team displayed. I'd yell, "Team!" and they'd shout back, "Together we will!"

The team had quite a journey to even make it to this game, so I wanted to make sure the experience was special. I had asked the local high school coach, who many of these kids aspired to eventually play for, to meet us to give the team a pep talk on game day. Early that Sunday morning, he met our team at Caitrin's Rock, with his two little kids in tow. Before he started speaking, the boys got up and explained what the rock was and what it meant to them. By the end, the coach was in tears listening to these kids talk. I'm sure he had an idea that morning about what he was going to say, and we caught him completely off guard. His speech probably went from something like, "Let's go out there and get them, boys," to "You guys have already won."

"What you're doing right now by honoring this little girl is truly amazing. Your camaraderie is every coach's dream. You've already accomplished so much," he said. He wrapped up the speech with, "Well, since you've come this far, you might as well go out there on the field today and finish the job."

We rented a bus to take us to the university we would be playing at. As we pulled into the parking lot, we saw the opposing coaches and team outside their bus. The looks on the kids' faces said everything. They were ready.

As soon as it started, it became apparent this was going to be one heck of a game. Both teams seemed to be at their best—playing physically, playing with heart. At the end of the first half, we were losing by seven. I remember being in the locker room preparing to give my pep talk. Just from a quick glance around the locker room, I knew it didn't matter what I said. It didn't faze them that they were losing. They just wanted to go out there and finish the game.

The second half, our team really dominated the clock. We had a big drive and were able to make it to the end zone to score a touchdown. With the score 6-7, the coaches needed to make a big decision: go for two for the win, or go for the extra point to tie it up. I knew we might not get another shot to get all the way down the field again. Looking at the kids, I knew the momentum was on our side. I knew that we might not get another chance, but I learned from business that you might not always be right, but you have to take the chance. I paused and looked at the other coaches to get their input on whether we should go for one point or two, and they were all 100 percent aligned to go for two.

The play started, and our quarterback rolled to his left. Just as he was about to throw the ball, he got hit by a defender, and his throw wobbled in the air. I held my breath as number 87 popped up between two defenders and caught the ball. I swear the moment was so surreal. We ended up winning 8-7. It wasn't one player, one play, or that moment that won the Super Bowl for us. It had been a miraculous journey, an evolution over the course of the season.

At the end of the game, the president of the league gave me the game ball. Typically, the winning game ball will go to the coach or to a player on the team who made a big play. We determined immediately that the ball was going to go to Caitrin's family. This really resonated with the commissioner, and he asked me to go over and talk to the Bartlett players before they left. I walked over to our opponents, huddled up, heads a little down. I said, "You guys played a fantastic game. I want to let you know that our team set out with a purpose this year and that wasn't to beat you or to win this game. It was to honor a little girl who passed away in our community. There are no real losers or winners today, because in the end, what really won out is the idea that if you play for something bigger than yourselves, when you are competing for anything in life, you can achieve great things. This game ball isn't going on someone's mantle somewhere as a symbol of 'beating Bartlett.' It is going to the little girl's family." As I talked, the heads that were hanging low popped up. By the end of the talk, I had eye contact with every kid in that field, their gazes filled with the understanding that this was about something bigger, about something more.

A BIGGER PURPOSE

Earlier, I wrote about our *why* exercise, the ultimate outcome of which was the realization that Medix already had a profound goal: to place people in jobs that fit their skills sets, which has significant financial, personal, and other implications.

Once we came to that realization, we formulated a phrase to articulate our purpose: "Positively impacting lives." And while the *why* exercise revealed that our purpose was to have an impact on talent, we decided to extend beyond that to encompass teammates, clients, and communities.

Equipped with that idea, we set a goal of having a positive impact on twenty thousand people, guided by four points:

1. Seek to place candidates in roles that will allow them to thrive and achieve their professional and personal goals.

2. Seek to have an impact on our clients by understanding their objectives, fortifying their teams, reducing turnover, enhancing performance, solving business problems, and helping them to achieve their goals.

3. Have a positive impact on our internal teammates by locking arms, cultivating and growing one another, showing up for one other in times of celebration and in times of sorrow, and helping one another reach our full potential.

4. Make a difference in our communities through volunteerism and philanthropy.

UNVEILING OUR PURPOSE

We strategically chose our national kickoff meeting as a forum for unveiling our new purpose. I wanted to roll it out in a way that would resonate with as many people in the company as possible, and I knew that would take more than a conference call. Each year, Medix flies in teammates from across the country to Chicagoland for a few days of uniting around vision and goals, development and training on key initiatives, and camaraderie and team building.

The morning was filled with good sessions in which various facilitators from our company talked about trust and the importance of working in teams, team building, sharing, and collaborating. In the afternoon, we broke into groups of six to ten, and big boxes were brought into the room. I watched nervously as our teammates shot hesitant and skeptical glances at one another, wondering what crazy plan we had concocted this time. What made the plan even slightly crazier was that we had only had a couple weeks to pull off the planning of this activity prior to the meeting. I had been at an industry conference two weeks prior, soaking up everything I could like a sponge (per usual). While chatting with a peer of mine, Andrea, she began to describe a company she had used before for a truly impactful team activity. As she was talking, light bulbs were going off in my head; I knew this was it. This was the perfect way to hammer home our core purpose (never mind the tight timeline)! After some frantic phone calls organizing everything with the team and with the company, we were actually able to line everything up. We were going to pull this thing off.

The teammates tore into the boxes to find that they were filled with parts for kids' bicycles along with tools to use in building those bikes. I joined the attendees and, per instructions by the facilitators of the exercise, we mixed everything up. We took screws and tools out of some boxes and put them into others. Then the clock was set, giving us an hour to assemble the bikes.

The facilitators began to guide the groups in collaborating to put the bikes together. People were scrambling to find the tools and parts they needed. I was the designated tool guy, so I had handfuls of tools and I was running from group to group, letting the team members select the tools they needed to build the bikes.

All along, the clock was ticking, one hour…thirty minutes… fifteen. With five minutes left, we had a set of brakes that wouldn't go on one of the bikes, so team members from other groups rushed in to help.

The alarm went off and we broke into a round of applause, partly because we felt a sense of accomplishment but also because we felt a sense of relief. It was collaborative and fun, and we felt we had succeeded in doing something special.

The facilitator asked, "Okay, what does a bike represent?"

"A bike is freedom," someone answered.

"A bike is transportation," another person volunteered.

The facilitator asked, "What did you do today?"

We had learned how to work together in teams, how to collaborate, and how to share. It was refreshing and invigorating to see the goals we could achieve when we worked together.

With everyone still gathered around the bikes, I got up in front of the group and started talking about the concept of making a positive contribution to other people's lives.

"What you folks do day in and day out is about a lot more than putting bodies into seats, just as what you did today was about more than assembling a bike," I said. "When you're doing what you do every day, it's easy to lose sight of the greater impact you're having on people."

We talked briefly about the broader meaning of building the bikes—that a bike was more than just two wheels; it was a vehicle for a child to experience freedom and independence.

And then the doors of the conference room swung open and a group of kids from the local Boys & Girls Club came in to retrieve their bikes. Boys and girls alike filed into the room, first apprehensive and uncertain about what to expect from a room full of businesspeople in suits. Anxiety melted away as the children ran to the stations where the Medix teammates stood with their bikes. Our team helped them onto the seats, rang the bells on the bikes, and talked to the kids about home, school, and life. The kids were very excited and talked to team members and gave them thank-you cards. In interacting with the children, we found out that most of them had never had a new bike, or any bike for that matter.

A number of people in the room teared up because it was such an unexpected, emotional surprise. Everyone assumed the bikes would be donated after the event, but I wanted the team to be able to experience the effect of their efforts on these kids. I wanted them to see the expression on the kids' faces, to hear their voices, to physically hand them the bikes and see the immediate emotional impact on these children, up close and personal.

And I wanted to help them connect the dots: I wanted them to see how helping someone get a job could produce ancillary experiences like the one they were witnessing. We can't always see the joy on children's faces when they receive a new bike, but we can imagine the positive impact of helping someone land a new job, the grown-up's version of getting a new bike.

Then I put up a slide of our old, outdated BHAG of earning $1 billion in revenue and said, "This is no more. Our new BHAG is about having a positive impact on twenty thousand lives. The old BHAG was about our success, and the new one extends to helping others achieve success. And today you got a chance to do it, see it, feel it, and touch it. Now I want every one of you to go back to your offices and bring it to life."

I hoped that the bicycle exercise would drive home the idea that every time Medix staff members sat down to interview candidates, they should think of a way to make those candidates' day a little better, make them feel valued. For the candidates, a new bike may be the furthest thing from their mind. They are focused on more urgent matters, such as putting food on the table. The bike-building exercise was a perfect vehicle for showing the connection between what we do at Medix and how it can positively affect lives in ways that we may not always be conscious of.

My Medix team was really moved by the bike experience. They still talk about it to this day. And I try to do similar activities on a regular basis to reinforce that we truly can make a positive difference to the lives of others. A core purpose activity is now part of every kickoff meeting. We devote an afternoon or evening to some kind of activity to drive home our core purpose. For instance, one year, we put on a surprise magic show for a little girl and her family. The child had a neurological disorder and the show was in support of the Make-a-Wish Foundation. After the idea came to me, I brought it to the team that was helping plan our national meeting, and they really ran with it. We invited our local teammates' children to come join us. The team found an actress to stand in as Ariel from *The Little Mermaid*, the little girl's favorite Disney character. They found out the little girl's favorite foods and organized a buffet for all of the kids. They filled the conference ballroom with balloons and streamers in the little girl's favorite colors. No detail was missed.

The little girl entered the ballroom on her crutches and you could see her light up. She had no idea what was going on. She thought that she was simply there for a magic show. The look on her face was nothing compared to the look she had when, at the end of the magic show, we brought her up front and let her know we would be sending her and her family to Disney World. We were so happy to have the opportunity to do something positive for this family, but the impact on our team was significant too. It was another instance of sending our teammates home after having touched and felt our core purpose so they could bring it back to their Medix offices and continue to weave it into the culture.

FROM CORE PURPOSE TO CORE VALUES

Along with the identification of our purpose, it was important to reevaluate our official core values. While Medix's core values had long included sterile terms such as *accountability* and *professionalism*, they evolved, in 2012, to become:

- desire to serve others

- willing to do what others won't

- never, never, never give up

- locking arms to achieve our goals

While we had always had these values deep down, we found ourselves needing a way to promote organizational cohesiveness so that we could enhance engagement and drive our purpose of having a positive impact on other people's lives. With an organization of hundreds of teammates spread across the country, we needed to promote that ideal of a single, connected team. So we developed the idea of "locking arms to achieve goals" as a way of visualizing what it means to be linked to one another as a team, and we added to that the never-say-die spirit of giving it our all, of "never, never, never giving up." This was done in the same spirit as defining my football team's motto of "Together we will." The same principles applied to coaching kids and running a major company: we needed a cohesive and bonding focus in order to win.

Through the success we had in bringing the core purpose to life by building bikes at the national kickoff meeting, we decided to use themes and activities to bring our values and organizational goals to life as well on a quarterly basis. Just as the bike exercise did, themes really animate our folks and encourage friendly competition among teams, and prizes are usually linked to team bonding or philanthropy. For example, a recent theme was Medix Jeopardy, in which offices competed to increase our talent net promoter score (NPS), which is a leading indicator of growth in our industry and a key metric for our company. That quarter, each office had a Jeopardy board listing questions relative to the staffing industry, Medix history, and general Medix trivia, and the winning office got to donate its earnings to its philanthropy of choice. By playing this game, teammates nation-wide engage in friendly competition while working to achieve a key business objective—driving NPS, in this case—and simultaneously making philanthropic contributions throughout the year while adding to our overarching BHAG at the same time.

There are innumerable examples of our core values in action in our offices across the country. For instance, Shea in our Dallas office once got a call at 4:00 p.m. on a Friday from a valued customer who needed thirty people for a project starting on Monday. If our Medix team had given up and gone home for the weekend, this could have been a disaster. Instead, Shea called Steve, the office leader, who said, "Don't worry. We've got your back."

That unified approach changed everything. There they were, on a Friday afternoon, with a last-minute request to deliver thirty people basically overnight. The weekend was within reach, and here was an unexpected glitch to their personal plans. But nearly everyone from that office showed up on Saturday and Sunday and pitched in to fill that job request for the client. Their teamwork ensured that thirty people reported to work on Monday morning for our satisfied client.

But don't take my word for it. Here is what some of Medix's people have to say about what it means to live our core values:

> "Recently, we were awarded a lucrative six-month, twenty-person, Windows 7 migration project at a major health system. While we had confidence in our IT recruiter, Jeff,

we knew it was a tall order for just one person since we had never worked in this fulfillment space in the Rockville market. Brian, who has a lot of experience selling in IT, stepped up to take it on and created a solution for the customer. Without being asked, Cole, one of our science recruiters with aspirations to become an account manager, also stepped up. For an entire week, Brian, Jeff, Cole, and I locked arms and worked long hours every day until all twenty were signed on. This is the kind of culture we have at Medix: when the chips are down, we do

what it takes to help each other succeed. I'm excited to have these guys on our team."

—Steve, Sales Manager, Rockville, Maryland

"The team in Boston is doing things that truly reflect our core values while rapidly growing a business together. After a period of hard times, the team really peeled back the onion to look at who we are, what Boston wants to be known for, and what culture we want to build. Things finally started to take shape. We had a new 'us,' a renewed vision and purpose, and most of all, team members who

were committed to each other. We started doing lots of team-building events in and outside the office, we focused on the fundamentals of the job every day to get better at it, and we sought and found new business that would offer the growth we wanted to have. We now know what it means when we say, 'locking arms to help each other achieve each other's goals; desire to serve others; never, never, never, never giving up on each other and our dreams; and being willing to do what others won't.' We're truly doing something special here and we're excited to create opportunity for others as we move forward."

—James, Sales Manager, Boston

"Locking arms extends beyond just our own teammates, and locking arms with clients doesn't just mean helping them with business objectives. When it comes to showing appreciation for our clients, material items don't seem to go as far as they once did. Our biggest opportunity to gift our clients today is getting involved in their organization's philanthropic events. In recent years, Medix has placed a focus on joining our clients in having an impact on our communities. For example, we have locked arms to participate in a client's cancer awareness walk, fundraised for an ill child, and even volunteered to take calls for a cancer telethon. Our clients have a great appreciation for our involvement and interest in supporting causes that are important to their companies, and they have netted tangible business results and stronger partnerships."

—Valerie, National Sales and Delivery Manager

"A great individual example of our core values is our AZ teammate Karl. He picked up his life, moved to Denver for two months—didn't ask for a dime, by the way—and locked arms with our Denver office to help them achieve an all-time high. His second weekend there, when a teammate had to drive to Wyoming to pick up furniture from her boyfriend's house, he immediately said that he had never been to Wyoming and that he would drive and help her out (her boyfriend was in Canada). He truly believes that he will grow professionally in this company by having an impact on lives. I have no doubt he will continue to have an impact on our company and people year in and year out."

—Casey, Executive DBO, Scottsdale, Arizona

"Nick B. was willing to be shipped to Redlands, California, with essentially zero notice, and he laid the foundation for great relationships to be built within a top client to help our company grow for years to come."

—Sean, Sales Manager, Nashville

"Nathan K is the embodiment of the core values: developing through our internal growing pains (never, never giving up); taking whatever role/territory was put in front of him (desire to serve others, willing to do what others won't); helping to open *three* different markets; and working in *five* (locking arms). He has displayed all core values in spades through his career here. He has been an integral part of the company's growth."

—Eric, Managing Director, Medix IT

"I met Medix's CEO, Andrew, at my friend Casey's birthday party. That was the first impression I had of Medix: his CEO was at his birthday party! It wasn't long before I found myself in a corner of the room learning about Medix from Andrew. The passion for his company and what they were building was amazing. He then asked me to stay an additional day to 'shadow.' So I delayed my trip home and came in to work on Monday with my friend Casey.

The following week, Medix offered me a position in Arizona. I took the job for the same reason I am with Medix today. It's a high-energy, coaching, growth-minded, team-focused, family environment. Medix is a place that cares not only about you as a teammate, but more importantly, you as a person. Medix is less focused on where you are today and more focused on where you can go. I am very honored to be part of such a great organization aligned in such strong values and purpose."

—Ken, National Director of Care Management

We lock arms to help each other achieve goals every single day. From the first day you start work at Medix or go on the road to sell to a customer, you know that you have teams all over the country you can rely on to pitch in if you need help to make something happen. Often, a company's core values or mission are just words on a web page or in a brochure. Not ours. We live and breathe our values and purpose. And when it comes to having a positive impact on others' lives, our authenticity is off the charts, deeply felt, and carried out by everyone in the organization.

In many cases, having the purpose and values that we do has helped us win business: our purposeful work is impressive on its own, and clients simply want to be associated with it. But oftentimes, it goes beyond that. Our genuine interest in having a truly positive impact on business means clients understand that we don't need to "be right." Rather, we are more interested in uncovering the right answer or putting together the right solution that will honestly solve our clients' challenges. Say you're a hospital that has contracted us for help with a long-term implementation of electronic medical records. You can have a high degree of confidence that everyone who touches your project will be dedicated, responsible, conscientious, and tenacious in getting to know your objectives and making sure you reach them. We have high-value customers who know they can rely on us if they've just closed a deal with their own customer who wants to be up and running within forty-eight hours and needs last-minute teams of quality personnel. And year after year, I've watched our teams work diligently to meet requests—high volume, short notice, and everything in between—happen for their teammates. Each individual Medix office is a family who bonds together for the greater good—and we'd been "locking arms and never, never, never giving up" way before we adopted these core values.

TOUGH DECISIONS GO DOWN EASIER WITH PURPOSE

At Medix, we aim to interact with teammates and talent in a way that considers their body, heart, mind, and spirit in order to make them feel valued, respected, and trusted. Our teammates work here because they want to make a living, of course. But at the same time, they appreciate the environment and support embedded in our purpose-oriented culture. And if people experience a period when work is less than satisfying, our purpose can help motivate them to stay the course.

We've also found that having solid core values makes it much easier to figure out who fits into the organization—and who doesn't.

Probably because of my early career experiences and the feeling that I lacked sufficient mentoring, I tend to pour my heart and soul into coaching people and am reluctant to give up on someone even when it's clearly time to let go and move on. For instance, recently, a teammate who had been high performing hit what I hoped and thought was simply a rough patch. In spite of my encouraging and coaching her through second, third, and fourth chances, the teammate didn't turn things around. When measuring her against the core values and purpose she used to embody, I could see some of that had faded. Inevitably, we had to part ways, something a lot of companies would have done long before I did.

Unfortunately, it's clear from a manager's, customer's, or colleague's feedback that some teammates do not share our core values or aren't living our purpose, and we have to consider letting them go. Even if they are high producers delivering $2 million to the bottom line, if their values and purpose aren't aligned with the organization, we must decide it's time to part ways. Purpose must take precedence over everything, even over profits. If it doesn't, it won't be long before the mismatched goals will be apparent to teammates, the trust will be lost, and the consequent emotions and feelings of disparity that can surface may really begin to dent morale.

THE RESPONSIBILITY TO DO GOOD

Most people think they're building their business to make money. Obviously, that's a component. But when you start a business and hire workers, if you really start to pay attention to what's going on with them, you'll find out you're in the business of taking care of people and their families. Think about it; everyday life for a lot of people is no picnic. At times and in different stages of life, it can get pretty tough to make a go of it, to make ends meet, to keep a family safe and warm. Do you really want to create a work environment that adds to these challenges? I'm betting you don't. I wanted to create a work environment that offered a respite from the difficulties life can sometimes throw at us.

If you have enough gumption to start a business, you should have enough foresight along with that gumption to create a business with purpose and core values that are good for your people and add some joy or hope to their lives. In our line of business, we get the opportunity to do this for both our internal teammates and our contract talent.

CARLA'S STORY

Two of our recruiters, Jake and Steve, were working with an applicant named Carla. She interviewed well and had a dynamic personality and a good background. We had recently adopted our core purpose, and Jake was committed to placing her. At one point, Jake became a little skeptical about some inconsistencies he was noticing in Carla's address and phone information. Something didn't seem right. Nevertheless, Jake didn't give up on her.

After about four months, Jake found Carla a temporary job at a hospital that was a client of ours. She performed so well there that they offered her a permanent position.

About a year later, we contacted the talent we had placed at the hospital to ask if Medix had had a positive impact on their life and we asked them to tell us their story.

Carla sent us a video in which she said, "Hey, Medix, I'm going to tell you something you didn't know. When you were talking to me about a job for almost five months, I was homeless. I was living in a car and having a very tough time. I didn't tell you, because I was embarrassed. Over those months, you never stopped calling me. I felt valued. You gave me hope. And then you changed my life."

"My daughter," she continued, "who had been sick for many years, passed away. Because my living situation was so unstable, [the state] sent my daughter [and] my granddaughter to Atlanta to live with my other daughter. When I got a temp job, I was able to rent an apartment. I worked hard and was offered a permanent position. I started saving money so I could visit my granddaughter and daughter in Atlanta. I got my career on track and now I want to become a medical coder. I am so grateful to you guys for sticking with me and helping me get back on my feet."

We asked Carla to come in to share her story with the Medix team at one of our national kickoff meetings. When she finished her talk, we presented her with some surprises. We told her that when she was ready to go back to school for her coding degree, Medix would pay for it and thus help her increase her annual salary by a minimum of $17,000 and probably a lot more. We also gave her a round-trip plane ticket to Atlanta so she could visit her family. That is that gumption I was talking about earlier.

It's amazing. Once you figure out your company's purpose, everything else falls into place. Purpose has transformed our company and, most importantly, it's authentic.

CHAPTER 7

MAINTAINING A WINNING TEAM

Maintaining a purpose-driven team requires not only attracting the right people who embrace the right mentality but developing your strategy around engaging them and playing into their strengths. For example, the year our Golden Eagles team won the football championship, we started with a jet offense, but that strategy requires a super-fast kid, and we didn't have one. So we changed our playbook to run a double-wing offense to fit the players on our team. It was about first assessing our teammates and building them into the very fabric of our strategy.

Getting the "who" right at Medix was a major stride. Even if you have the perfect strategy, you still need to understand who's on your team and what skills they have. This is imperative when implementing new ideas. We keep a list of innovative ideas that pop into our heads, and they routinely get a rigorous once-over for their cost/benefit value. For each great idea we consider adopting, we want to know we have the human capital fit to enable us to execute: people with the right skill sets and aptitudes to make the venture succeed.

Deciding what we choose to do and not do is done carefully in light of the capabilities of our teammates.

"Seeing the kids play as they did through-out the season, learning to play as a team and how everyone mattered—it was inspirational. As a parent, I saw all the things you want to see in a team sport. There wasn't one player making plays all the time. It was different players, playing to the best of their ability and gaining each other's respect and trust. Players weren't overcommitting to make up for a weakness. They trusted their teammates to play their position and fill their gaps. It was truly a great season and great accomplishment for all of our kids."

—youth football parent David

We also enter new markets based on positive indications from our market research and whether we have a champion or client in a particular region, along with the right team member to spearhead the launch and hire staff who fit the Medix profile: competitive, team oriented, and aligned with our purpose and vision. Opening a new office requires significant resources—time, energy, heart, and soul, to name a few. So we need teammates who embrace our purpose and who are willing to go the extra mile to ensure success. We also make a commitment to provide the office leader with the support and resources he or she needs to grow.

DEEPEN YOUR BENCH

Whether in sports or in business, the key to versatility and agility is having a dynamic bench. If you thought the hard part was over and your job is finished when you have a team stacked with A-players, whether in business or on the field, you thought wrong. Just as important as the team you have in place is the network of professionals you have in your pipeline. Life happens. People leave organizations. Organizations outgrow people. Players move on. Players get hurt. To adapt, you need to be able to throw your weight around.

This is why networking is so important. Look at the circle of people you surround yourself with. You might be surprised at the skill sets you have hidden in your cell phone contacts or in your LinkedIn connection list.

FIRE (OR DON'T HIRE) A VENDOR WHO DOESN'T FIT

The partners you choose, as a leader, are part of your "team." You must determine when a vendor is a bad fit. It is commonly accepted business wisdom that's it's okay to "fire" bad customers, the ones who don't contribute that much to your bottom line but cost you money (and give you grief) in the process. So I took a similar bold step with a company I determined was a "bad" vendor.

In 2015 I went to a charity golf outing in Houston. The night before, a number of invitees were at a sports bar. One was the founder and CEO of a prospective Medix software vendor, with whom I sat and talked for a bit. He asked me, "Hey, Andrew, what differentiates you from your competition? Why are you guys different?" So I proceeded to tell him about our value proposition and how we were able to come up with new and innovative solutions to solve the problems of our clients and talent. "But the real difference between Medix and other companies," I added, "is that every fiber of our being lives and breathes purpose and values. Ask any of our teammates about how our purpose to 'have a positive impact on lives' pervades our culture and motivates us to be the best at what we do."

Now, admittedly, the guy had probably had a few too many drinks by that point, but in response to my enthusiasm, he said, "Listen, Andrew, I get it. You're trying to come up with some kind of marketing ploy to get your teammates excited so you can make money. But come on. We're both CEOs. You can't pull the wool over my eyes, buddy."

I shook my head and walked away, reminding myself of the authenticity of Medix: I've seen our team shovel gravel and hammer nails for a wounded veteran who needed help with his house. I've seen them raise money for cancer research, for granting kids' dying wishes, and for a talent whose house was robbed right before the holidays. I've seen them give purely out of the desire to help others without a thought to what they or the company might get in return. We earnestly look for opportunities to help people. And our team is genuine about it. They want to be part of making a difference, and they willingly jump right in and help wherever they can.

About six months after the encounter in the bar, I was reviewing proposals from vendors who responded to an RFP we had put out. One was from the software company whose CEO I'd walked away from in Houston. I dismissed the bid outright, based on that incident. And the sad thing is that his company had a great solution. But I absolutely could not bring myself to do business with the guy because I knew how little he aligned with Medix's core purpose and our way of doing business.

Instead, I took our business to a different vendor and banked on its ability to deliver the features and solution we needed. It was a gamble but one I was comfortable taking because I'd heard the winning company's CEO speak at a conference earlier in the year, and I was very impressed by how transparent he was and by his story about purpose. On the podium, he actually admitted that his company had not been providing good service to its clients but that the company was committed to changing. I appreciated his honesty and integrity.

So even though I strongly preferred the first company's solution, I decided I would rather work with the second company's attitude. We were already using one of that second company's solutions, so we took a chance on adding another solution from that company and we haven't regretted the decision.

A WORLD OF COACHES AND MENTORS

Another way we maintain a high-performing and purposeful team is by fostering a culture of mentorship. For a true winning team, it's important to have people to lean on, and different mentors serve different purposes, personal and professional. Some mentors help check emotions and perceptions. Others might be experienced businesspeople who can give advice and help maintain focus. Others might be people to bounce ideas off or help organize thoughts.

Often, mentors give their services for free. It's amazing how many people just want to help, especially if those needing help are authentic and have humility. If you have these qualities, you'll meet scores of people along the journey who can be a lifeline when you need it.

In fact, we've found that coaches and mentors are everywhere—in YouTube videos, TED talks, chance meetings in the café. During Medix's first ten years, I had a mentor named Dave Kolb whom I met at The Swamp, a little restaurant in the lobby of our building. I was drawn to his personality, and he ended up being someone I would call if I was stuck and wanted to talk. What began with a handshake ended with him becoming Uncle Dave to me. I could be talking to him about private school versus public school for my kids. I could also be talking with him about the changes in healthcare and how it might affect my business. Whether talking about business or personal issues, I could rely on Dave. To me, he is the epitome of what a mentor is.

At Medix, mentoring is the primary way we foster professional development and build leaders within the company. We firmly believe that mentorship helps promote innovation, and we want mentors who are open minded and encourage the expression of ideas, no matter how off-the-wall they may sound.

Mentoring at Medix happens formally and informally. It's embedded in our culture. Over time, we formalized the Penholders Group program that eventually became the Mentor Program we have today. Through the program, we pair newer teammates with more seasoned people, and the mentor is there to talk about anything, be it business or personal. The mandate of our formal mentoring program is to increase our number of mentors by helping the person next to you become as competent as you are or more so. Grooming people to take on new responsibilities has enabled us to successfully open new offices and launch new products.

Two key purposes of our internal mentoring program are to allow our senior teammates to have a positive influence on the newest members of our team and to give our mentors exposure to leadership and coaching as a way for them to prepare for future leadership roles in the company. The program is designed to align experienced, accomplished teammates with newer teammates to establish weekly mentoring sessions, in which the mentor coaches the mentee on best practices in meeting preparation, development, opportunity management, and situations that occur unexpectedly. Another part of the process is having the mentors share their coaching experiences with their peers and an "executive sponsor." These conversations serve the purpose of group collaboration and help shape the leadership techniques of the mentors. This is the part of the program in which the leadership coaching takes place.

TRANSPARENT REVIEWS OF THE EXECUTIVE TEAM

Having all the right stuff—and making sure you keep it—comes from really taking a look in the mirror, so to speak. It's not enough to fill your key seats with A-players; you need to constantly evaluate the health of the team to make sure you spot areas where players might be struggling or could be challenged even more. You need to be able to look for instances where your team might have outgrown a member or, vice versa, where any team members might have outgrown their role and are ready for increased responsibility and challenges.

To do that, our leadership and executive teams do reviews of each other—no holds barred. In our humility-minded culture, criticism is delivered graciously and taken for the learning opportunity it is. We all understand that if someone has something to work on, it's likely others have a similar issue. So each leader's review is a group-learning experience: what might be happening in an office in New Jersey can be instructive for the folks in Orange County.

The executive team also has individual meetings with their regional directors to review the feedback they receive so they can devise an action plan together. From our feedback, we distill one, two, maybe three things we can use to improve ourselves.

In addition, the leadership team gathers two or three times a year to review the feedback everyone provides anonymously about their superiors. We do not reveal names; it's an open forum in which an office leader can say, "I'm experiencing this and I see a couple of other offices have received similar feedback. How are other people dealing with this?" So in effect, leaders are getting coaching from their peers and senior execs simultaneously on how they can be a better leader.

Again, it's all anonymous, but because we are such a transparent, cohesive group, people often end up raising their hands to claim and clarify their input. So I may see an anonymous comment such as "Andrew has a hard time letting someone go when it really is time. He should make decisions like this faster." And someone will speak up and say, "Hey, Andrew. I said that and I was talking about this specific situation." In many organizations, you'd never reveal that you were the one who had critiqued the CEO. But it's not like that at Medix.

With our we-all-coach-each-other mentality, people generally don't get defensive but are more likely to say something such as, "I didn't realize that. Can someone help me understand more where that is coming from and how I can fix it?" It's important for teammates to be receptive to feedback and appreciate where it is coming from, and people are often willing to come forward to explain their own remarks to help clarify if it will help their peers.

ATTRACTING BIRDS OF A FEATHER

As a leader, as an individual, you must be aware of what drives you, what gets you up in the morning, what allows you to be authentic. Picture yourself sitting on the edge of your chair, talking to someone about your passion, and they're saying, "Oh, boy, wow. I get it. I see how much you believe in this."

If a company can identify its purpose—why it exists and what it's all about—the right sorts of people will be attracted to the organization. Job seekers will say, "That company is a fit for me."

Purpose can help you overcome difficulties. Things aren't always easy, but when you understand your passion or your purpose in life, it grounds you. When Medix discovered its core purpose of having a positive influence on others' lives, it was the most rewarding time in my life. A multitude of things just fell into place. It has helped make it effortless to do whatever I do, personally and professionally, because I know why I exist. When you understand why you exist or what drives you, it's unbelievable what it can do for you.

It isn't necessarily about hiring people who have the same personality as you or the same opinions as you. We are not interested in building a company of clones. Differences in perspective and experience are what makes a company versatile and poised for continuous growth, but the core of what you stand for should be unified. Building your winning team truly boils down to attracting the right talent, locking arms with the right partners, reflecting on areas for development, and mentoring one another to grow together as an even more cohesive and powerful team.

CHAPTER 8

ENGAGING AND EMPOWERING

As Medix evolved into a company that truly placed purpose over profit, we wanted our people to realize it wasn't just lip service. I wanted our teammates to be involved in our philanthropic initiatives and in our processes and to get more involved with our company on a personal level. It was not enough to declare our purpose on a corporate level; our teammates needed to see it, feel it, embody it, and drive it on their own. To feel like they had ownership to truly drive our purpose, they needed to be empowered and engaged.

Once we realized the importance of teammate engagement, we decided to work with an outside consultant who could guide us and help us make necessary adjustments to processes in a timely manner. And I can say without exaggeration that it has been an absolute game changer for us.

The primary vehicle, which I mentioned earlier, is the weekly, one-question, TINYpulse teammate engagement survey that measures internal NPS. We also use a virtual suggestion box to obtain recommendations from teammates on an anonymous basis about things they would like to see implemented or changed, anything from a marketing idea they would like explored to recommendations on coffee types for the break room.

While we are accountable for responding to comments and communicating our responses—positive and negative—the key is *how* the message is delivered. Our method is to issue a weekly report on the company's overall NPS score that includes some of the comments and suggestions. There is no stupid question or suggestion. We respond to every one and implement the suggestions that make sense for the business. And we don't just fill the report with good comments; we include comments from people who are unhappy as well. It's all done in the spirit of complete transparency.

At the end of the year, we recap and share the information company-wide. We include all the good and the positive things that we implemented, and we share the things that people are unhappy about. We tell them what has been recommended and what we did about issues that generated a lot of feedback. The report also breaks down individual offices so leaders are fully in the loop. If teammates feel they are submitting ideas and suggestions but are not being heard, they will, over time, stop responding altogether. By demonstrating to our team that we are both listening and acting, we are empowering them to continue to play a vital role in evolving our company.

When it comes to performance reviews, millennials want regular feedback in small chunks. They don't wait for yearly performance feedback; if there's something they should be doing differently, they want to know now. That makes perfect sense to me, so all teammates have weekly informal feedback sessions with their managers. These sessions are called DEFTs, which stands for discipline, execution, feedback, and training sessions. Teammates across the country group up with their peers and leaders selling in the same industry to instill motivation and share knowledge, and the results have been great. A teammate selling in the healthcare revenue cycle space in Arizona will give tips to a teammate having trouble setting a meeting with a revenue cycle client in Chicago. A care management leader in Dallas will go through virtual role-plays with his team, which spans the country, from coast to coast. It really ensures we are learning from challenges and successes across the country, staying sharp on important issues and topics in our industry, and showing up to help teammates on the other end of the phone whom we may never have met in person.

For new teammates, we have more formal six-week and twelve-week reviews to ensure they stay on the right track. Later, we shift to annual reviews. We encourage people to ask for feedback on demand if they need to, but we find that the weekly DEFTs are very effective.

Our teams in the field huddle three or four times a day. The whole office may do this, or individual divisions or teams may huddle. In huddles, people get feedback, coaching, and a chance to refocus, which has been an exceptional way to communicate.

HAVE YOU CONSIDERED COMMUNICATING WITH MILLENNIALS?

In his book *Turn the Ship Around!* David Marquet talks about his approach to empowering and speaking with millennials and, really, all teammates, for that matter. We've adopted it and have found it to be very productive in promoting a self-starter mentality throughout our largely millennial workforce. So instead of saying, "I need you do to this," a manager might say, "Have you considered doing this?" "Have you considered that if you approach the task this way, you might have a better result?" And the teammate may answer: "Yeah, I did consider that. Did you consider this?"

Or if we are certain we're going to do something, we say, "I intend to do these things. Are you good with it?" The theory behind this is that we are now giving permission to teammates to contribute to management. It's more of a bottom-up management style that I believe has had a big impact on our culture. For an executive team, to be that vulnerable and relinquish a bit of control can be intimidating: What will the teammates say? What if an executive disagrees with the teammates' sentiments? Before stifling that engagement and grabbing the reins back, we try to take it as an opportunity for collaboration. We do not always have the perfect answer, so being able to empower teammates to arrive at the best answer for the company *together* with executives has allowed us to multiply leaders in our organization. It may sound as if this methodology will waste time; if you, as a manager, know the answer, wouldn't it be more efficient to explain it and move on? In actuality, while you might save a couple minutes giving the answer rather than letting your teammate work his or her way to it, you still end up losing weeks and even months of productivity by not scaling your team to be fully engaged and to make decisions themselves as opposed to operating on autopilot. Scaling a team of self-starters who can work independently will outpace and outwork one manager who knows it all any day of the week.

MEDIX FIT: SOMETIMES YOU SWING, AND SOMETIMES YOU MISS

Through our engagement software, we aimed to uncover the true motivations of our teammates, what they really cared about. Medix Fit was part of our objective to turn Medix into a company where millennials loved to work. In 2013 we were inundated with teammate feedback about long work hours that interfered with people's efforts to get to the gym. In response, we rolled out Medix Fit—our Fit for 100 initiative—with a lot of fanfare.

In addition to paying for every teammate's gym membership, we sent everyone in all of our offices Medix gym bags, water bottles, and Medix dri-FIT T-shirts. And we said that on two occasions, every week, teammates could have the flexibility to leave the office an hour early, come in late, or take an extra hour at lunch to go to the gym. We also encouraged people to have Medix Fit outings on the weekends and share their Medix Fit stories. The Arizona office sent pictures of the team climbing Camelback Mountain; Houston sent a picture of a group playing dodgeball. They got points for sending in Medix Fit stories.

But not all teammates understood the policy well, and sometimes, communicating it properly got "lost in the sauce" when we were growing at least 20 percent year over year. So, many folks did not use it in the way it was intended. A lot of teammates were angry and wrote reviews complaining that their office leader wasn't giving them their Medix Fit time.

In practice, this new company policy of empowering teammates and giving people two hours a week for the gym was a nightmare for office leaders and for our efforts to apply it uniformly across the country. It put office leaders in a tough spot when business pressures interfered with their attempts to accommodate requests to leave for the gym. For example, an office leader might have said something to his regional leader such as, "I know you want me to hit my goal. A customer called us at 3 p.m. with ten critical requirements and two of my best recruiters just took their Medix Fit time. This is crazy."

We ended up modifying the policy by eliminating the two hours off per week. We still paid for the gym membership but realized we needed to give our office leaders the flexibility to reward their people with time off on a case-by-case basis when it was called for. If one week, everyone was working 7 a.m. to 7 p.m., maybe the following week they could be rewarded by being allowed to leave early one day and come in later the next.

In addition, we started asking our office leaders to create an environment in which teammates felt comfortable coming to them with a comment such as, "Hey, we just finished two twelve-hour days and feel really good about where we are in terms of meeting our goals. Do you mind if we bolt at 4 p.m. today?"

So the time-off part of Medix Fit turned into a debacle. We learned that in an organization the size of ours, once you offer a perk like that, you can't take it back without negative repercussions. People wonder why the perk was given them in the first place. It comes across as empowering them but not trusting them. In actuality, we needed to do a better job of defining empowerment within parameters that made sense for the business. When we altered the policy, we had to be careful not to point fingers at people for not following the policy in the way it had been intended to be used. It was tough. Since then, when we consider a big initiative, we commit to not taking it back later on. We organize a focus group to explain what we're hearing and ask whether that is what people really want or whether they'd prefer something else. And we work with them on crafting alternatives.

Motivating and engaging your team isn't an easy task. Even when you have the best intentions to make your team happy, you might still be met with anger—and that's okay. Engaging teammates is a fluid process that takes vulnerability, transparency, and sometimes a little trial and error.

CLIENT AND TALENT ENGAGEMENT

When we monitor our effort to have a positive impact on lives, we make it a priority to ensure that not just our teammates are engaged and productive but our talent and clients are engaged as well. After all, they are an extension of our Medix family. We prioritize discussion of the feedback we receive from our customers and talent, using NPS surveys on a regular basis. This keeps us in the loop about a range of issues that detract from the customer experience. Whether it's a change in a business process or a personal gesture such as sending a birthday card, congratulating talent on a milestone anniversary, or sending a Starbucks gift card "just because," Medix teammates are encouraged to form relationships with talent and clients in a way that differentiates us from other staffing companies and fulfills our purpose mission, keeping them fully engaged and motivated to continue our partnership.

 "When Medix recruiters Dan and Arthur came to our first meeting, they were prepared with solutions, including a willingness to go above and beyond. They were always quick to respond to requisitions and gave me strong candidates. Dan and, later, Nick, shared feedback on our work environment that their talent had shared with them and brought to light issues that I had no idea about. At the time, our company was undergoing a lot of changes, and I was asked to take on more responsibilities. Medix was instrumental in helping me manage my workload and keep the pulse of the people on my team. Not long afterward, I decided that all our department's staffing needs would be handled by Medix. Medix helped me grow my department, improve morale, and increase revenue. They helped me win in an environment that was presenting many obstacles."

—Molly, current Medix consultant and former executive with a Medix client

EMPOWERMENT ON THE FIELD: HOW WE BROKE OUR FOUR-GAME LOSING STREAK

Heading back to the football field, I discovered that giving people the opportunity to provide input on new directions also works outside the workplace.

After the football team I was coaching had racked up four losses in a row, I started thinking about a different approach and took a step back. Instead of huddling with them to try to motivate them, I decided to let them huddle on their own. I put the responsibility on them and reminded them that we coaches couldn't win their games for them; we couldn't get on the field and make the blocks and tackles and throw the ball. They had to self-motivate. Just as managers cannot do all of their teammates' jobs for them, it was important that the team find the motivation within themselves and took ownership of their game.

So the kids huddled. They leaned on their peers and themselves for motivation and direction. I have no idea what they said to each other, but whatever it was, they believed in it and they owned it. We won the game and broke our losing streak.

It just goes to show that people, regardless of age or walk in life, have great ideas and a great desire to make a difference in their own lives. Sometimes all they need is the space to make those decisions and the tools and encouragement to do so.

CHAPTER 9

PURPOSE UNLEASHES INNOVATION

During our championship season, #32 was one of the best players on our team. During the playoffs, he broke his wrist in a game against one of our opponents. For a different team that perhaps centered on one or two star players, this could have been a devastating blow to the season. Instead, our team had purpose, and that purpose was "Together we will." We had built our strategy around the team, not individuals, and were thus able to innovate. During our next game, after his injury, the opposing coaches were talking about "trying to stop #32," not knowing he would not be playing. They were shocked when they saw him in a cast. What resulted was that our team adapted by throwing the ball more than running it and seeking different ways to move the ball and score.

When we made it to the championship game, he was suited up but wasn't going to play, still stuck in a cast. When we hit a point where we knew we were going to win, we put him in for one more play. Even though we were able to innovate and push the season forward past his injury, he was a big reason for our making it to the championship game in the first place, and he deserved time on the field just as much as the next guy. It was a great moment when purpose met innovation and success.

If your company is focused on profit and pushing product, it severely limits your ability to innovate. Innovation is key because the world is dynamic and ever changing. The second you feel yourself growing comfortable, you are already behind. Technology forces innovation. In our world at Medix, healthcare reform forces innovation. Drug development forces innovation. In a world where nothing is stagnant, you need to be constantly thinking two steps ahead.

"The director of IT at a large provider of print, digital, and supply chain solutions with a sizable contract said there was something different about me and Medix and that's why he gave us a shot. He said we showed sincere interest in their business and that we were determined to find out what would work for his team. We listened to what they looked for in talent and what worked on his team, specifically. We didn't win the business from the first meeting (it was two quarters later). But I followed up with him often and think I did that (and still do) because of our core purpose. I don't want to be your average vendor. I want clients to trust that I'll be a true partner in helping them succeed."

—McKenzie, Account Executive, Medix Chicago

When we found out what our true core purpose was and we went into every conversation with the goal of having an impact on our talent and clients through whatever means necessary, we completely changed the game. By listening to ideas from across our organization and from the mouths of the very clients and talent we serve, we've been able to continually develop new and better ways to improve our services. Instead of trying to convince clients and talent of what's going to work for them, we completely shifted our business model to what would positively impact them. And if we don't have a service that matches the need, we'll look at ways we might innovate and bring in something new.

As a staffing company, the business model seemed standard across the industry. A client has a need. The staffing company finds a person to fill that need. Thinking about who Medix truly was, and collaborating with mentors like our business consultant, Steve, we realized that this didn't have to be our story. Medix has a unique purpose, and we could have a unique model. Steve truly pushed us to innovate and helped us to change the conversation, both with our clients and internally. When our conversations with our teammates shifted from being solely, "Did you hit your numbers?" to "Did you impact that person or solve their problem?" we were able to create new, more efficient, more effective business models. This resulted in higher profits, happier talent and clients, as evidenced by climbing NPS scores, and a more engaged internal workforce empowered by the fact that they were not only selling or recruiting but solving problems and impacting lives.

At Medix, we're now able to see whole new service offerings, whole new worlds that we never even considered looking at before. By *listening* to clients and talent, we find better ways to serve them. Today Medix is a top player in the industry, thanks in part to some of the innovations that we've implemented. Examples of some of the innovative solutions we've been able to develop through listening to clients, talent, and our own personnel include:

Medix Intelligence℠. This is our proprietary screening and interview methodology that uses data to provide higher intelligence and information on our candidates to ensure more effective hiring decisions. We launched Medix Intelligence because we understand that there is so much more to evaluating a candidate than a resume and standard interviewing protocol. Armed with the ability to make better hiring decisions, clients are able to reduce turnover and meet business objectives while also helping place talent in ideal opportunities where they will thrive.

"Steve, manager of our Texas office, had met Talehia on a plane ride to Dallas and referred her to us. Her expertise was in call centers, but she did not have any healthcare experience. Nevertheless, we had conviction in not just her abilities but her soft skills and aptitudes. We pitched her to a client where they historically have only hired people with healthcare call center backgrounds, but we just knew she would be a great fit in that environment and would quickly pick up on the experience she lacked. Guided by our core purpose, we succeeded in placing her on a temporary basis. Then, before her contract was up, she was offered a permanent job."

—Kristen, Professional Recruiter, Medix Chicago

Medix Match® is a solution that takes our application of Medix Intelligence a step further. It allows us to not only do a more in-depth screening of hard and soft skills of the talent we are submitting to the client but the ability to benchmark the top-performer profile and cultural fit of that specific team and submit candidates who match the unique fabric of the organization.

MedixDirect®. When the Affordable Care Act was enacted, hospitals nationwide were scrambling to find people who were trained to handle medical records and could also operate the various technology platforms of electronic medical record systems. There was a stark shortage of this talent. We took a look at the issue to identify our clients' challenges, and by asking what the client needed and wanted, we assembled a team that locked arms and put together a solution to create and train talent in this space, impacting talent through enhancing their careers and clients through helping them solve their deficiency of certified HIT talent.

By applying our purpose to every decision and being open to innovative ideas that unlock better ways of doing business, we have contributed directly to the health of our bottom line. We are just plain better at our jobs. We don't just fill vacant positions with anonymous faces; we really care about our clients and talent, and we work to understand their goals and pinpoint their challenges. And then we commit ourselves to solving problems by placing talent in positions that help them and our clients succeed. It is this tangible impact, this being part of something bigger than business, that keeps our internal team coming back into our Medix doors every day and going above and beyond on nights and weekends, knowing it's tied to a purpose they can see with their eyes, feel in their souls, and truly believe in.

CHAPTER 10

EMBRACING "OHANA" AND LIVING "TOGETHER WE WILL"

As I reflect on the tangible and intangible impacts purpose has had on business and my life, it all comes back to this idea of family.

While on a family vacation to Hawaii, I was introduced to the concept of "ohana," which means blood-related family as well as people whom you informally adopt. When hearing this, I immediately thought about my Medix family.

The early years of Medix were unconsciously filled with this concept. The Medix team circa 2002—Nate, Patrick, Chris, and Phil—were all connections from childhood, family, or college. We all worked well together and shared the same work ethic and a high degree of trust. The camaraderie was intense. They were there for me for everything from recovering from a bad client meeting to grieving the loss of my mom. They truly had my back, which has turned into one of our taglines.

The camaraderie has only gotten stronger. In fact, we embrace the idea of ohana within these walls every day. To us, family includes everyone we spend time with in our lives, creating a strong bond and an unspoken expectation that members will cooperate with and remember one another. Ohana is at the very core of our culture and provides a strong foundation on which to build our team directives and our service delivery.

Serving companies and talent is how we positively impact lives, so going the extra mile to match the right person to the right opportunity is part of our DNA. This takes time . . . and energy. Many of our teammates work long hours five days a week. Occasionally, they are even asked to come in on a Saturday or Sunday to meet a deadline. It is just the demands of the business; if a client needs people to come into work tomorrow, it means our team is working tonight.

Our culture is not for everyone—people who are focused on individual goals don't fit in here. At Medix, you're expected to give your all for the people you serve and the teammate sitting next to you. You have to be willing to go the extra mile for teammates, talent, clients, and causes. We want people to love coming to work. And it has a multiplier effect that positively impacts a lot of lives. It's all about the team, just like the greatest football teams in the world.

OHANA ON THE FIELD

We had the opportunity to bring the idea of ohana to the football field during the year after our Super Bowl winning season. "Together we will" had been such a unifying motto the season prior, and we knew the true power of having a rally cry that our team could stand for. That year, the motto the team selected was in fact "Ohana," to embrace the idea that they were a family marching toward a common goal. Like before, the team used this to fuel them each and every game. One game we played was against the Bloomingdale Bears, once again a team that had actually beat us the year prior but whom we ultimately bested on the road to the Super Bowl. Three days before we were to play the team, the Bears' head coach called me and informed me that the team's quarterback had lost his father; the man had died after a fall at a construction site. The family had been planning the funeral, and although the quarterback initially wasn't going to play in the game, he changed his mind. "He wants to play for his dad," the Bears' coach told me. My immediate reaction was, "How can we show up? What can we do?" So we decided we would do something memorable as an organization; we wanted to honor the quarterback and his father in some way.

Before the game, both teams gathered around Caitrin's Rock; it was the first time we had invited another team to join us in that ritual and to share the message that, no matter what, we were just thankful for the opportunity to compete. Our kids were genuinely in the moment for this player. Then we all walked onto the field together, literally hand in hand. You can't find a truer image of ohana than that.

The game went really well and we were ahead; near the end of the game, the Bears were at our fifteen- to twenty-yard line. With seven seconds left on the clock, there was time for one more play. The Bears changed up their positions: the quarterback went to wide receiver and the wide receiver went to quarter-back—they wanted to try to throw the ball to the boy who had lost his dad.

The wide receiver (as quarterback) threw the ball, and the player who lost his dad jumped up out of nowhere and caught that ball at about the three-yard line. He fought through our team, and through his sheer force and will, he carried the ball straight to the end zone for a touchdown.

It was amazing. Our staff, our players, our fans, their fans—in that moment we all got it. Even our coaches—I'd never seen a coaching staff cheer for players on another team! We got what this game was all about and had a clear moment of understanding why people play sports.

We talked to our players after the game about doing the right thing. Everybody on our team knew that wasn't a gimme. What happened taught our players and me a lesson of truly positively impacting lives. It was an amazing, profound experience and a touchdown that I'll never forget.

We felt really lucky to be wearing jerseys that day. And wouldn't you know, there's a photo from that day with a ray of sunshine streaming down on the team. You couldn't have staged a picture like that if you tried—it was very special, almost spiritual.

EXTENDING OUR MEDIX FAMILY: POSITIVELY IMPACTING OUR COMMUNITIES

Believe it or not, what keeps me up at night these days is not whether Medix is going to hit our numbers (with a tenacious team like ours, that's easy) but how we can multiply this notion of togetherness and ohana and extend our impact into the community.

When opportunities arise to provide and share these amazing experiences, we make them count, no matter the cost. Recently, we heard about a Gold Star widow who was about to lose her house if she didn't pay her delinquent note to the bank. The woman and her children had raised $2 million for multiple military charities because her family's own story had gone viral over the Internet, but she had donated the funds to help others instead of helping herself.

We contacted her right away and suggested that she come and do some work for Medix in exchange for an advance to pay off her mortgage. We also partnered her with Charlie, a Wells Fargo financial advisor and fraternity brother of mine to help her establish a budget and serve as a resource for her. She was overjoyed and has positively impacted Medix through her story and her work. But there's never a "wink-wink, nudge-nudge" when it comes to Medix's giving. We don't do it with the expectation of winning business. Sometimes our teammates don't even know about something we've done. It is genuinely about doing things that can make a difference in someone's life. We do these philanthropic endeavors because that's who we are at our core.

Camp Hometown Heroes (CHH) is another perfect example of partnering with an organization to do amazing things for others who need it most. CHH is an organization in Wisconsin that helps seven- to seventeen-year-old children of US servicemen and women cope with losing a loved one in combat or through accident, illness, or suicide. As a cause, it really spoke to us because we are passionate about helping children. The group running the camp is also an amazing bunch of people; their values and purpose align so closely with ours that it was a natural partnership.

At our kickoff meeting that year, we challenged each Medix office to raise enough money to send one out-of-state child to camp. Each Medix office came up with its own activity for raising money— one office did a poker game, another did a beanbag tournament. In true Medix spirit, teammates jumped onboard without being asked, poked, or prodded. We raised $30,000 in four months—enough to send twenty kids to camp.

We also locked arms with another fantastic organization to help wounded veterans. Football fans recognize Jared Allen as a very well-regarded defensive lineman that has played for the Minnesota Vikings, Carolina Panthers, and other teams across the NFL. He was doing some business with a neighbor of mine in Scottsdale, and we struck up a conversation. Years later, he embarked on a USO trip to US military bases in the Middle East, and he realized that he had to do something for the veterans. Shortly after, he began Jared Allen's Homes for Wounded Warriors, a nonprofit dedicated to rehabbing homes for wounded vets. He was still playing football but transformed his life through his philanthropic work and realizing his own purpose.

In October 2009, before we had formalized our purpose of positively impacting lives, Jared called to ask if Medix would help support his foundation. I said without hesitation, "Yes, absolutely." We didn't realize the impact this would have on us until we started meeting the vets, and then we were inspired in jaw-dropping ways. Our support includes sponsorship of Helping Heroes events to raise funds for the nonprofit; when they are able, our local teammates in Arizona also participate in home-build events near the office to lend their hands-on support.

> "I feel so fortunate for the support Andrew and his Medix team have extended to JAH4WW. It's not every day you have the opportunity to join forces with a corporation whose values match so strongly with what we are trying to do with our foundation. I'm so thankful and proud of what we've been able to build with partners like Medix."
>
> —Jared Allen, retired NFL defensive lineman and founder of Jared Allen's Home for Wounded Warriors

Formalizing our purpose and making it part of our DNA has helped us look at our own lives a little differently; we now appreciate more in the day-to-day. From a business perspective, it has the added benefit of attracting the kind of teammates we want to build this organization, particularly millennials who need to feel they are making a social difference. Many new hires tell us they were drawn to Medix by looking at our Facebook page and seeing all the things we do to support causes. Same thing with clients; time and again we hear that we were chosen because "I like what you stand for and what you are doing." This is priceless to us because veterans and their families are truly part of our ohana—they share many of the same values, the same DNA, and the same purpose.

THIS IS WHO WE ARE

Like teaming up with fantastic partners in our communities, I feel very fortunate to have had the opportunity to work with other purpose-driven people like our business coach, Kevin, and youth football coach, Bob. I got lucky in life running into them and others who want to help people see the bigger picture. They've helped me to put together game plans and strategize and try to position the team to execute and succeed, but more importantly, to develop a purpose and a life lesson to be learned.

At a recent youth football banquet for my team, I had one message for my kids: "Have courage to be who you are." Simple, right? "Have courage to be the one who opens the door for someone. Have the courage to give up your seat for an older person who comes to watch a game—a mom or dad or grandparent. Don't be concerned about what your peers will think of you. Have courage to surround yourself with the right people."

As a team member or an entire organization that is growing and developing, you must have courage, purpose, and strong values that always keep you together. On the football field, we are continuing to innovate, evolve, and fine-tune our skills, all while minding the important lessons of team building we are instilling in these young kids. As we continue to grow and multiply as an organization, we want to make sure that everybody knows we're one company, one team. Yes, our customers are important. And yes, the talent that we place is important. But what's more important than anything else is how we show up for each other, day in and day out, through the good times and the tough ones.

It's just like on the football field: I want the parents and kids to know that when they're coming to bust their hump in practice, it's a safe place for them to be genuine. They can have humility. They can have trust. They can have balance. They can be open. They can learn life lessons.

"TOGETHER WE WILL"

Finally, I want to return to the motto of "Together we will," which came about from the life of Coach Bob Ladouceur who led the De La Salle High School football team in Concord, California, to a record-setting 151-game winning streak. Their story is depicted in the film *When the Game Stands Tall*. After we made that the motto for our football team and I brought the kids to see the film, I was so inspired that I had every office in the company arrange to see it as well. Then I invited Coach Ladouceur to come speak at Medix's national meeting and invited my entire football team and coaching staff to come, too.

While Coach Ladouceur spoke to us at our meeting, I realized what an honor and a privilege it was for me to see the joining of those two teams that were such an integral part of my life—my football family and my Medix family. And it made me realize more than ever that I am a coach—every day, in every aspect of my life. He was so kind and genuine that he even took time out of his schedule to share a moment at Caitrin's Rock with us.

"My son played every game for everyone else on the team but himself. He did not want to let anyone down. He learned that he was there to play for the guy next to him and that no matter what he had his back. This created a great sense of camaraderie. It created a brotherhood amongst my son and his fellow players, a brotherhood which he respects and carries with him on and off the football field."

—youth football parent Angelo

It was a powerful moment for me as a coach, to reflect on how the kids respond to constructive influences around them. They quickly adopted the "Together we will" concept when it was formed and showed us adults the meaning of the phrase in ways we never even fathomed. But it was also powerful to think of myself as a player on these teams, someone who must continually learn from everyone I encounter, including football players and coaches, clients and candidates, Medix talent and clients' talent, and my peers here at Medix. Being human-centric at every turn is the only path to sustainable growth. We are driven by the value that "Together we will" means we can achieve anything if we work toward it as a unified front.

Once Medix figured how to create this unified front all those years ago, the job of incorporating purpose into our organizational fabric turned out to be the easy part. Call us lucky that we had it in our DNA, or call us enlightened that we were humble enough to acknowledge that we needed help.

Having come as far as we have, I think that companies that work continuously to build an engaged, motivated workforce—whether through articulating and living a meaningful purpose or in some other consequential way—at best are leaving profits on the table and at worst will see significant negative ramifications in all organizational corners.

But the remedy is actually very simple, and in essence, it's unrelated to all that you were likely taught in business school. It's about the people—it's caring about what happens to others and how your dedication to more than the bottom line can make the world a better place. In short, it's about being committed to and living your values, and for us, that means "Positively impacting lives."

 "My son taught me a great lesson yesterday and this morning. I was talking to him about almost scoring from the one-yard line yesterday and wondering if he called out the wrong play. He said, 'Mom, we were all offsides.' I said, 'So-and-so's mom said he jumped offsides.' Cade said again, 'No, *we* all jumped offsides.' Then he said, 'Together we will.'

I realized what he was saying without saying it. I'm completely humbled by this team. Wow is all I can say. This is an incredible group of boys who really care about each other. Together, we were victorious long before the final game."

—youth football parent Tonia

CONCLUSION

WHAT'S NEXT?

Wrapping up this book is hard. For someone who loves to talk and tell stories as much as I do, it is difficult for me to put a cork in it even on a normal day. But what makes summing this book up particularly difficult is that the *stories never stop coming*. Every month, every week, every day, the Medix team is engaging in some action that just further paints the picture that purpose truly trumps all.

On the football field, we continue to motivate our teams with annual themes centered on more than just winning. One year's theme was "Ohana." The next was "One with purpose." We are still forging deep roots of teamwork using a myriad of methods, not just with running drills. This year, we kicked off the season by taking the boys to clean up a local bird sanctuary. We set the tone for the season before they ever even touched a football.

At Medix, we still are living and breathing our core purpose day in and day out, and it's just as alive today as it was when we first rolled it out. And the continued success has followed suit. Our TINYpulse engagement scores are at an all-time high. We continue to invest in innovation to reinforce our services and respond to client and talent needs. We stay true to the Gazelles methodology to keep ourselves accountable and on track. Our clients and talent continue to feel valued and supported by the team, with our NPS earning us spots on lists citing the best of staffing clients and best of staffing talent. We continue to receive accolades from industry publications highlighting our growth rate. This year, we will post impressive numbers for a 30 percent growth.

And beyond those facts, we also sent twenty-three kids to Camp Hometown Heroes this year. We continue to wear pink and raise awareness for breast cancer in October and brandish our best mustaches and raise awareness for men's health in November. We continue to feature a core purpose activity at our national kickoff meeting, year after year. This year, in fact, our team had the opportunity to explore the similarities between unified teamwork and making music when we brought in the Chicago Philharmonic Jazz Orchestra. Our team then witnessed the impact Medix had when it presented new instruments and scholarships for music lessons to children in the youth orchestra. There were very few dry eyes in the house. We are already thinking about what we are going to do for the year after that (and the year after that!).

That's why it is hard to put a cap on the book. We are still fully in forward motion. Purpose is so engrained in our culture that I know every day there will be new examples to demonstrate the power of purpose. The beautiful thing about purpose is it never runs dry. This story has no end and is always "to be continued." And for that, I am infinitely grateful.

ABOUT THE AUTHOR

Andrew Limouris is president and chief executive officer of Medix, a staffing and consulting company specializing in recruiting skilled personnel for clients in the healthcare, science, and information-technology industries.

With the mission of fostering a purpose-driven organization, Andrew found his niche when he started Medix. The Medix team grew and evolved organically through innovation, strong core values, and the inspiring core purpose of having a positive impact on people's lives. The organization has been featured on such prestigious lists as Crain's Chicago Business' Fast Fifty, *Inc.* magazine's Inc. 5000 list of the nation's fastest-growing private companies, and Staffing Industry Analysts' Largest Staffing Companies in the United States. Andrew was also an Ernst and Young Entrepreneur of the Year finalist in 2015.

Andrew is the son of Greek immigrants and credits his parents with his work ethic and how he treats people. Andrew graduated from Ripon College in 1994 with a bachelor's degree in speech communication. Today he resides with his wife and their three children in Illinois, where he is impassioned by coaching youth sports and looking for opportunities to create an impact on and off the field, at home, and at work.